English # Heritage

Conservation Areas in the North of England

Graham Pearce
Les Hems
Brian Hennessy

First published 1990
ISBN 1 85074 258 8

THE CONSERVATION AREAS OF ENGLAND

VOLUME FOUR

THE NORTHERN COUNTIES

Including the counties of:-

Greater Manchester	Cumbria
Merseyside	Durham
South Yorkshire	Humberside
Tyne and Wear	Lancashire
West Yorkshire	Northumberland
Cheshire	North Yorkshire
Cleveland	

Copyright©Historic Buildings and Monuments Commission for England 1990

First published 1990 by
Historic Buildings and Monuments
Commission for England
Fortress House, 23 Savile Row, London, W1X 1AB

Printed by The Dorset Press, Dorchester

ISBN 1 85074 258 8

CONTENTS

	Page
Introduction	vii
The Basis for Action	vii
The Pattern of Conservation Areas	xiii
Conservation Areas in the Northern Counties	
Greater Manchester	1
Merseyside	8
South Yorkshire	12
Tyne and Wear	17
West Yorkshire	20
Cheshire	29
Cleveland	36
Cumbria	39
Durham	44
Humberside	48
Lancashire	52
Northumberland	59
North Yorkshire	61
Glossary of Terms	71

FOREWORD

Growing public interest in our built heritage over the last twenty years is reflected in the way local authorities throughout the country have been active in identifying areas of historic and architectural character. This has not been an academic exercise but an expression of planning policy and these areas -**conservation areas** - are formally designated with precise boundaries, with a view to the preservation and enhancement of their character. For this purpose local authorities have been given special planning powers. Starting with the 1967 Civic Amenities Act which required all local authorities to identify and designate conservation areas, the number and size of conservation areas has grown steadily over the years, but most rapidly in the mid 1970s. By the end of 1988, there were 6,300 in England.

Some local authorities publish lists and brochures identifying their designated areas and explaining their significance and all provide information on demand. Formal notices are placed in the local press at the time of designation but, with the passage of time, people can lose sight of which localities have and which have not been the subject of designation. It is not easy for the public or local authorities to compare action in different parts of the country; nor can they easily obtain a picture of the kind of areas widely regarded as meriting designation.

In response to this need a national inventory has been prepared. This provides a comprehensive guide to all the conservation areas in England at the end of 1986. Supplementary lists give details of designations during 1987 and 1988. The inventory is published in four volumes each covering a different part of the country. In addition, a single volume national list of the names and dates of designations complete to the end of 1988 is available.

The inventories have been compiled using information on designation, scale of coverage and land use, supplied by individual local authorities in most instances. The maps were prepared by English Heritage. For post-1986 designations, extensive use has been made of the London Gazette, where all new conservation areas and amendments are advertised.

The preparation of the inventories has been a team effort and we owe particular thanks to Jenny Hipkiss, Julie Green, Pat Field and Debbie Evans, of the Public Sector Management Research Centre, Aston Business School, for their sustained efforts in logging information and for secretarial and graphics support.

Graham Pearce and Les Hems,
Aston University Business School,
and Brian Hennessy, English Heritage

January 1990

INTRODUCTION

The widespread designation of conservation areas in England over the past two decades signifies an important shift in public attitudes towards the built environment. During the 1960's it became painfully apparent that, if steps were not taken to afford protection, the character of our towns and villages would be lost forever. The means of protection was eventually introduced through the 1967 Civic Amenities Act, which placed a requirement on all local authorities to determine which parts of their areas were of special architectural or historic interest and to designate these as conservation areas. By the end of 1988 some 6,300 areas had been designated. This is a remarkable achievement and is a clear measure of the importance now attached to urban conservation.

It is in the light of this accomplishment that this and the companion regional volumes have been prepared. They each contain detailed information on the principle characteristics of all areas designated at the end of 1986, together with supplementary information for designations during the subsequent two years. As such they provide a comprehensive guide, and an opportunity for determining and comparing the pattern of designations and designation policy, at national, regional and local scales.

Each volume is in four parts; we begin by identifying what designation implies in terms of the range of measures which may be adopted to maintain and enhance the character of conservation areas, either through the application of financial and legal provisions relating to conservation, or through the use of a wide range of other mechanisms and resources. Secondly, we review designation practice, drawing upon the information contained in all of the inventories. The third section contains information, by county and district, relating to each of the conservation areas designated within the region covered by this volume. (See Figure 1). This is followed by a glossary which defines the terms employed in the inventory.

THE BASIS FOR ACTION

The responsibility for designating conservation areas was originally vested in the county councils and county boroughs. In 1974, it passed to the new districts. In the National Parks, the relevant authorities remained the county councils operating, where necessary, through special joint committees. In the Peak District and Lake District, designation continued to be handled by the relevant Planning Boards. In London, the City Corporation and London Boroughs generally took the lead although the Greater London Council had concurrent powers to designate, powers now resting with English Heritage. Urban Development Corporations also have power to designate. Few of these authorities, whether in London, in the metropolitan areas or in the shires have failed to use their powers at some stage, and many remain active in identifying areas of character and affording them the necessary statutory protection.

But designation of a conservation area is only a preliminary step and local authorities are encouraged to adopt positive measures at an early stage to maintain and enhance the character of designated areas. This implies a variety of approaches which must relate to the needs of individual historic areas and the buildings within them. Powers which focus sharply on the protection of specific buildings and areas, and which confer recognition of their merits, are crucial to wider policy aspirations. Likewise, loans and grants targetted at historic buildings and areas can act as a catalyst for wider action by implanting confidence.

In some areas the emphasis will be upon **protection**; in others upon **supportive** measures aimed, for example, at environmental improvements or traffic management or grant aid for the repair of individual buildings. In certain cases **regeneration**, involving the integration of a wide range of initiatives and funding sources, will be required. Here the economic strength of the area must be bolstered and new uses, or more intensive uses, be found for individual buildings, especially those at risk.

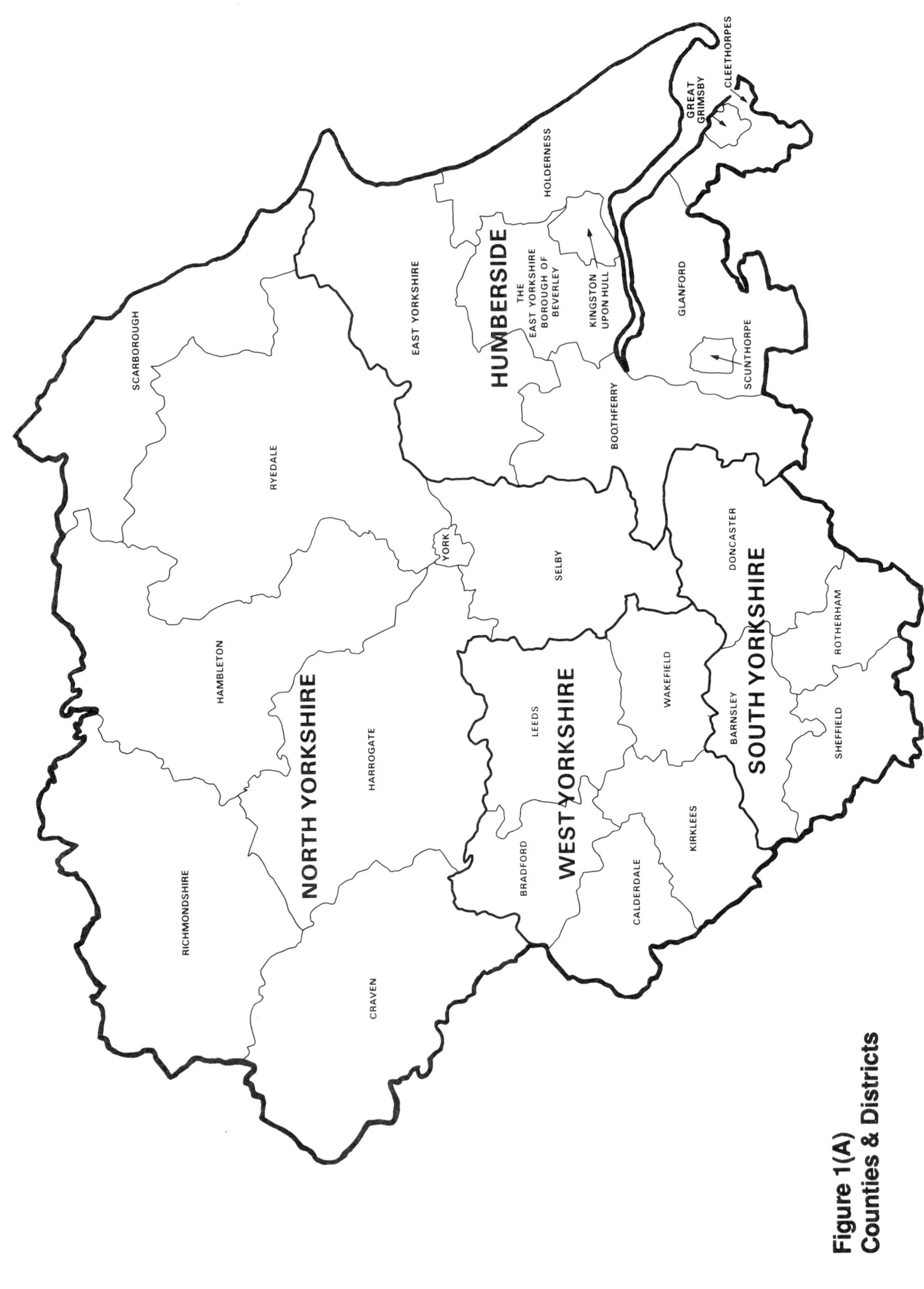

Figure 1(A)
Counties & Districts

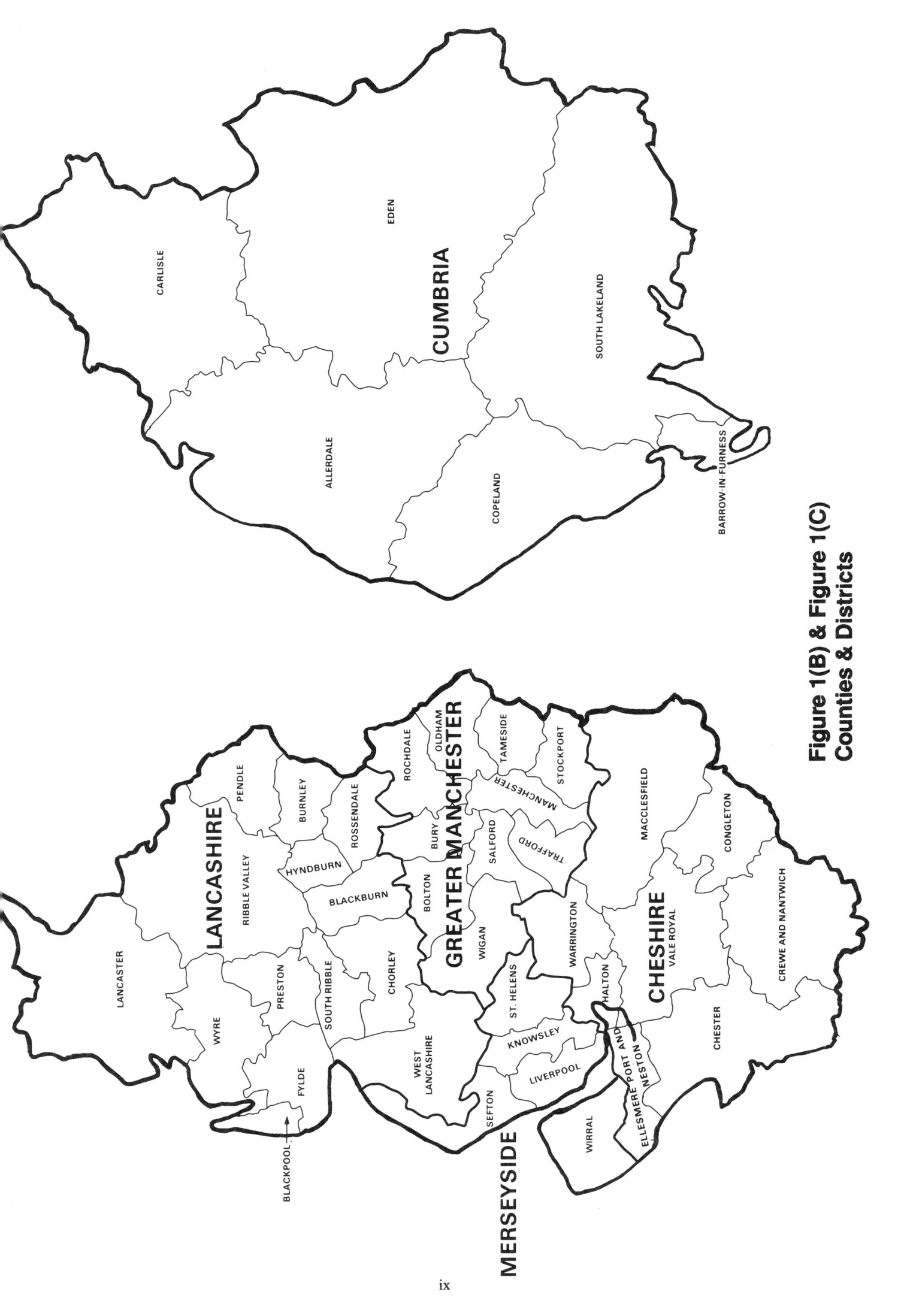

Figure 1(B) & Figure 1(C) Counties & Districts

**Figure 1(D)
Counties & Districts**

Protection

Conservation is therefore not merely a passive instrument; it implies action to protect and enhance. The local plan or unitary development plan will set the scene. It may contain proposals for the development of land within the designated area and provide for the diversion of harmful pressures for redevelopment. The plan may also include proposals for reducing traffic congestion in and around designated areas by traffic management schemes and road improvements, the provision of off-street parking and the introduction of pedestrian ways.

In addition to forward planning, control over new development may be strengthened in a number of different ways. For example planning authorities can require detailed plans and drawings of proposed schemes to be submitted, showing the development in its wider setting, instead of giving planning permission in outline form. Local authorities can also consider extending more detailed control over development through the use of an 'Article 4 Direction' where a special need can be shown to exist. Since 1974, the demolition of buildings in conservation areas has been brought under control. Conservation area consent must be sought for proposals involving the demolition of part or all of any building, other than a listed building. For the latter, listed building consent must be obtained before demolition, or even material alterations, can take place. Designation also extends controls over trees. Any person wishing to cut down or carry out work to a tree in a conservation area is required to give the local planning authority six weeks notice to enable the authority to consider whether to make a tree preservation order.

Because proposals for new development which are likely to affect the character of a conservation area may be of general public concern, local planning authorities are required to advertise such applications, and consider any representations they may receive in deciding whether or not to grant permission.

Supportive measures

Apart from protective measures, modest expenditure can achieve much, for example tree planting, the installation of well designed street furniture and removal of clutter. Moreover, a variety of conservation grants are available from central and local government, which are targetted at encouraging owners to repair their buildings where normal incentives are failing to operate. At the time of the introduction of the Civic Amenities Act, arrangements for grant-aiding groups of historic buildings had already been devised. These comprised 'Town Schemes' under which the Department of the Environment (later English Heritage) and individual local authorities jointly allocated a sum of money annually, to make grants for the repair of selected historic buildings. These qualifying buildings need not be listed but they must be within the conservation area.

The number of town schemes has grown steadily, from 58 in 1975 to 224 in 1988, the majority being in small and medium sized towns. The support required is dependent upon local conditions and the size of the historic area, and this may be reflected in significant variations in the pattern of expenditure, both over time and from one town to another. For example, in 1987/88 five Town Schemes, Bath, Brighton, Canterbury, Cheltenham and Spitalfields, accounted jointly for a fifth of the total Town Scheme budget of £6.6m. In contrast nearly 60% of schemes were allocated less than £20,000 and a fifth less than £10,000. The majority of grants are small in scale, but they provide a leverage effect, whereby the private sector and other agencies contribute at least 60% towards the costs of repair, and often much more.

Under the Town and Country Planning (Amendment) Act 1972, a new grant, generally referred to as a Section 10 grant, was introduced for action to preserve and enhance conservation areas where these were regarded as 'outstanding'. The grants were made by the Department of the Environment and, since 1984, by English Heritage. In practice the available funds have been focussed on larger projects than those assisted under Town Schemes. Grants normally amount to 25% of the eligible works. The identification of 'outstanding' conservation areas helped to ensure that the demand for grants did not outstrip the available funds, and that resources would be channelled into areas of national or regional importance. The requirement that an area be outstanding to qualify was removed in 1980 but other criteria, allied to limited funds, have resulted in Section 10 grants, together with town schemes, being concentrated in about 400 areas, mostly in town centres. In 1987/88 English Heritage offered £5.2m in grants under Section 10.

In order to co-ordinate and target Section 10 grants certain local authorities were invited to prepare programmes of work. The 'Programme' approach had its beginnings in the mid seventies when major historic towns like Bath, Chester, Cheltenham, York, Lincoln, Berwick and Kings Lynn began to prepare conservation programmes. But within a year or two the principle was extended to major Victorian cities and resorts - Bristol, Liverpool, Nottingham and Newcastle in 1977, Brighton and Hove in 1978, Hull in 1981 and Bradford in 1982. The funding allocation from English Heritage for programme towns in 1988/89 shows that of the £2.25m allocated, over 70% has been channelled into northern industrial towns - Liverpool, Bradford, Sheffield and Halifax and adjacent towns in Calderdale District being the principle recipients.

In addition to Town Scheme and Section 10 grants, local authority grants are awarded under the Local Authorities (Historic Buildings) Act 1962, towards the repair of historic buildings.

Regeneration and improvement

Apart from the adoption of specific provisions for conservation, a variety of other public sources of grant have been drawn upon in efforts to preserve and enhance designated areas. They are by no means exclusively for historic buildings, indeed many are not even specifically directed towards old buildings. They include funding sources whose overriding objectives are to foster employment and business and to improve housing conditions; but all may be applied, in appropriate circumstances, to the repair and reuse of historic buildings and areas.

Inner city policy: This is a collective term for a variety of initiatives aimed at dealing with a range of interrelated economic, environmental and social problems resulting from long term changes in the economic structure of our cities and older industrial areas. Priority is given to the fundamental need to revive local economies, to support enterprise and improve the environment in order to rebuild confidence and encourage investment.

Some 57 local authorities are currently involved in the preparation of inner area programmes and the potential for linking conservation to urban regeneration is therefore considerable. Finance may be provided for a wide range of projects including the revitalisation of redundant buildings and environmental improvements. Specific support is available for the conversion or improvement of buildings in industrial or commercial improvement areas, whilst City Grant provides encouragement for private sector schemes, involving the conversion and refurbishment of under-utilised and derelict buildings and sites, to provide accommodation for a variety of activities.

Housing: Local authorities provide limited financial support for houses in need of substantial improvement or structural repair. In the case of a listed building extra financial support may be available to cover the additional costs involved in securing its restoration. The Housing Corporation and housing associations are playing an increasingly prominent role in the provision of residential

Figure 2
Villages Designated as Conservation Areas

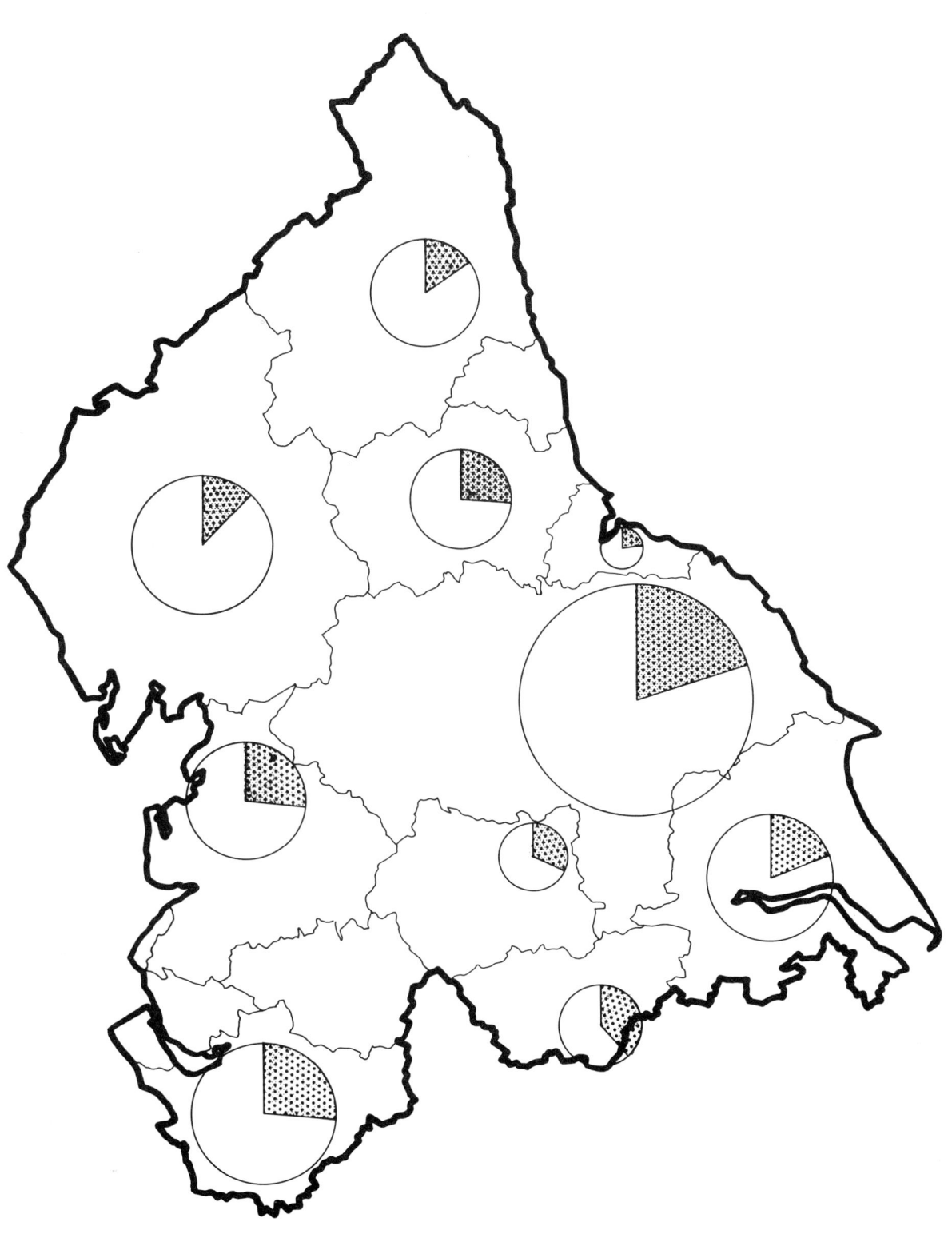

The shaded area represents the number of rural parishes where the main village is wholly, or partly, designated as a conservation area (prior to 1987)

The following categories are therefore identified:-

(a)   Urban areas

>London
>Towns/twin towns
>Urban villages
>Urban non-settlements

(b)   Rural areas

>Rural main settlements
>Rural other settlements
>Rural non-settlements

Table 2 shows that 2,373 conservation areas are located in urban areas and, of these, 489 occur within the main built-up area of London and 1,385 in towns outside London. Of the 3,560 designations in rural areas, 2,981 are located in the main settlements of civil parishes. These generally comprise villages or small country towns, bearing the name of the parish and possessing a parish church. Apart from these main settlements 497 designations relate to secondary rural settlements. Village designations account for a high percentage of the total since in addition to the main and secondary village designations in rural areas there were 367 'urban village' designations, giving a total of 3,845 conservation areas in villages. Apart from these main categories we find that 214 designations relate to 'non-settlements', implying an isolated topographical or built feature.

The geographical distribution of conservation areas, in terms of the types of settlement to which they relate, is shown in table 3. There are considerable variations in the incidence of designations from one county to another. Some counties contain fewer than 50 conservation areas, for example Northumberland and the Isle of Wight, whilst Kent has 321 and Devon 205 designations.

In part these differences are attributable to the variable size of counties and the pattern of settlements within them. Some counties contain an even spread of rural settlements whilst others are dominated by large urban areas. For example, whilst the majority of designations in the metropolitan areas are in towns (57%), in the shire counties over 75% of designations relate to village settlements. In some counties, for example Shropshire and Warwickshire, this proportion is even higher, 93% and 90% respectively. On the other hand in some other shire counties, for example East Sussex and Lancashire, the incidence of designations in towns is much higher than average; 43% and 39%.

In the absence of clear national criteria there are liable to be variations in the geographical pattern of designations which cannot be wholly attributed to such factors as the number of settlements. In order to test this we have determined the proportion of settlements, both urban and rural, which have a significant part of their centres designated. Of the 812 towns which possessed urban administrative status in 1974 table 4 shows that 576 (71%) had a significant part of their centres designated by the end of 1986 (see spatial coverage within settlements below). However, there are important variations in this pattern. For example, in the shire counties 78% of towns contain significant central area designations compared with only 50% in the metropolitan counties. Variations are also evident at the local level. Compare for example South Yorkshire and West Yorkshire, where the proportion of town centre designations are 38% and 71% respectively; or Cumbria with neighbouring Northumberland, where the number of town centres designated are 93% and 55%. This suggests that designation practice may be uneven.

TABLE 2:
Location of conservation areas by type of settlement and administrative area

Location	Greater London	Metropolitan Counties	Shire Counties	ENGLAND
London	489	-	-	489
Town	-	303	974	1277
Twin towns	-	46	62	108
Urban village	12	121	234	367
Urban Non-settlement	14	48	70	132
All urban	515	518	1340	2373
Rural Main Settlement	-	69	2912	2981
Rural Other Settlement	-	20	477	497
Rural Non-settlement	-	2	80	82
All Rural	-	91	3469	3560
TOTAL	515	609	4809	5933

Applying a similar approach to rural areas, the number of 'main settlements' designated can be compared with the total number of civil parishes. Table 4 shows that nationally 30% of all rural settlements have been designated whilst figure 2 shows the variation across the region in village designations. There are considerable variations in the designation 'ratio' from one county to another. The highest are to be found in West Sussex (63%), Surrey (62%), Kent (56%), Isle of Wight (53%) and Cambridgeshire (53%). By contrast the ratios in Cornwall, Cumbria, Lincolnshire and Northumberland are 15% or less. Such variations are particularly notable in the case of neighbouring counties, for example Kent and East Sussex or Warwickshire and Hereford and Worcester. As in the case of towns, the diversity of the pattern suggests that there is variation in designation policy amongst different local authorities and an analysis at district level would undoubtedly reveal even greater variation.

So far we have excluded Greater London from our analysis. This is because London has no administrative divisions which relate closely to its historic growth or urban structure. However, in an attempt to measure designation activity, on a basis similar to that already applied to the rest of England, the main shopping centres have been identified. Using these centres as an indication of 'town' status we are able to establish the incidence of designation activity. Of the eighty six 'urban areas', which correspond broadly to conurbation towns within London, we find that two thirds have their centres designated; this proportion is significantly higher than the average for towns in metropolitan areas.

TABLE 3
Location of conservation areas by county and type of settlement

	London/ Towns No	Villages No	Non-Settlements No	TOTAL No	%
Greater London	489	12	14	515	8.6
Greater Manchester	81	30	14	125	2.1
Merseyside	57	14	4	75	1.3
South Yorkshire	35	53	5	93	1.6
Tyne and Wear	29	8	5	42	0.7
West Midlands	56	13	15	84	1.4
West Yorkshire	91	92	7	190	3.2
Metropolitan Counties	349	210	50	609	10.3
Avon	36	52	2	90	1.5
Bedfordshire	11	68	2	81	1.4
Berkshire	20	54	3	77	1.3
Buckinghamshire	8	77	3	88	1.5
Cambridgeshire	20	146	-	166	2.8
Cheshire	38	93	7	138	2.3
Cleveland	17	14	2	33	0.6
Cornwall	18	53	4	75	1.3
Cumbria	23	53	7	83	1.4
Derbyshire	34	96	10	140	2.4
Devon	60	144	1	205	3.5
Dorset	20	83	2	105	1.8
Durham	8	49	6	63	1.1
East Sussex	35	44	2	81	1.4
Essex	44	128	3	175	3.0
Gloucestershire	17	98	5	120	2.0
Hampshire	61	149	14	224	3.8
Hereford & Worcester	26	97	4	127	2.1
Hertfordshire	24	107	13	144	2.4
Humberside	25	55	-	80	1.3
Isle of Wight	6	13	-	19	0.3
Kent	65	244	12	321	5.4
Lancashire	56	84	5	145	2.4
Leicestershire	27	136	-	163	2.7
Lincolnshire	25	92	1	118	2.0
Norfolk	31	158	9	198	3.3
Northamptonshire	16	95	-	111	1.9
Northumberland	9	26	-	35	0.6
North Yorkshire	22	172	3	197	3.3
Nottinghamshire	34	67	-	101	1.7
Oxfordshire	25	120	1	146	2.4
Shropshire	4	52	-	56	0.9
Somerset	31	81	4	116	2.0
Staffordshire	21	81	10	112	1.9
Suffolk	27	102	1	130	2.2
Surrey	36	90	4	130	2.2
Warwickshire	9	89	1	99	1.7
West Sussex	25	126	7	158	2.7
Wiltshire	22	135	2	159	2.7
Shire Counties	1036	3623	150	4809	81.1
ENGLAND	1874	3845	214	5933	100.0

TABLE 4
Designated settlements in urban and rural areas

	Towns		Rural main settlements	
	Number	Proportion designated	Number	Proportion designated
Greater Manchester	67	33	7	29
Merseyside	21	57	21	29
South Yorkshire	26	38	88	39
Tyne and Wear	20	50	7	14
West Midlands	26	62	13	38
West Yorkshire	51	71	63	32
Metropolitan Counties	211	50	199	34
Avon	9	44	124	31
Bedfordshire	9	100	120	50
Berkshire	7	86	101	44
Buckinghamshire	10	80	194	31
Cambridgeshire	13	92	253	53
Cheshire	20	65	271	26
Cleveland	14	79	26	23
Cornwall	21	71	180	9
Cumbria	15	93	272	12
Derbyshire	22	73	251	27
Devon	29	93	372	28
Dorset	14	93	261	25
Durham	14	43	150	26
East Sussex	10	90	106	32
Essex	28	79	265	38
Gloucestershire	7	71	254	31
Hampshire	17	82	234	44
Hereford & Worcester	13	92	424	19
Hertfordshire	22	95	112	62
Humberside	15	73	233	19
Isle of Wight	5	80	15	53
Kent	31	87	289	56
Lancashire	45	51	196	27
Leicestershire	12	75	276	43
Lincolnshire	15	80	533	15
Norfolk	14	100	531	28
North Yorkshire	15	87	778	20
Northamptonshire	14	57	252	35
Northumberland	11	55	152	15
Nottinghamshire	16	56	226	26
Oxfordshire	11	100	311	34
Shropshire	6	50	228	19
Somerset	15	93	316	21
Staffordshire	13	77	178	39
Suffolk	18	89	461	21
Surrey	18	67	71	62
Warwickshire	7	86	224	36
West Sussex	13	92	144	63
Wiltshire	13	100	261	44
Shire counties	601	78	9645	30
ENGLAND	812	71	9844	30

Historic Towns

It can be logically argued that designation should and does relate not simply to the number of settlements but to their historic character and that this may explain the variation from one county to another. In order to see whether this is indeed the case we have undertaken an investigation in which towns have been categorised in terms of their historic origins. About half of the 812 towns in England are 'pre-industrial'; that is they existed as towns prior to 1750. The pattern of pre-industrial towns covered by this volume is shown in figure 3. These towns were identified in a Council for British Archaeology report 'The Erosion of History', published in 1972. There remain 414 English towns which only became urban after 1750; here these are termed '19th century towns'. In addition some rural settlements were also identified as pre-industrial towns; here these are termed 'former towns'. In all, 339 'former towns', and five former town nuclei within existing towns were identified.

We are able to gauge the incidence of designations in pre-industrial and 19th century towns by identifying the proportion of towns in each group which had their historic centres designated at the end of 1986 (Table 5). (Figure 4 shows the variation across the region in town designations). The outstanding finding here is the consistently high proportion of pre-industrial towns which had their centres designated, 94% in all. A similar proportion of former towns have also been designated. By contrast, only half of the centres of the 19th century towns have been designated. Moreover, an assessment of the pattern of designations within 19th century towns at the county level demonstrates that designation activity has been far from uniform. For example, whilst 67% of the centres of 19th century towns in West Yorkshire have been designated, the corresponding figures for Greater Manchester and South Yorkshire are only 25% and 27% respectively. A similar variation is apparent in the shire counties, for example the ratio of 19th century town centres designated in Cleveland is 70%, compared with only 22% in neighbouring Durham. However, the final pattern of designations in 19th century town centres may not yet be complete. For example, whilst during the early years there was a preponderance of designations in pre-industrial towns, since the late 1970's there has been more emphasis on 19th century towns.

Spatial coverage within settlements

Maps showing the spatial coverage of each conservation area are produced as an essential part of the designation process. For obvious reasons it is not possible to include maps showing the extent of each conservation area in this volume. But in many cases the spatial coverage and location of individual conservation areas can be deduced from the description given here because we have identified the relationship between the conservation area and the settlement in which it occurs.

The assessment of the scale of coverage relative to the urban area as a whole presents few problems with respect to freestanding towns or villages. However, London is largely a single built up area and cannot be analysed in this way. Similar difficulties arise in the metropolitan counties; but here the urban form is generally more loose knit allowing the boundaries of individual towns or villages to be more easily determined. Conservation areas which relate to 'non-settlements' are necessarily excluded.

Table 6 shows that of the 1,385 conservation areas in towns, few cover the bulk of the town, but almost a third include the bulk of the town centre, and a further quarter encompass at least part of the centre. About half of the core designations in towns extend well beyond the centre to include, for example, adjoining residential areas. There remain 618 conservation areas which occur within towns but outside the town centre. Some are relatively large but two out of three comprise only small portions of the town.

In villages the pattern is quite different. Nearly half of the 3,845 village designations cover the bulk

Figure 3
Pre-Industrial Towns (in urban areas) National Parks & Areas of Outstanding Natural Beauty

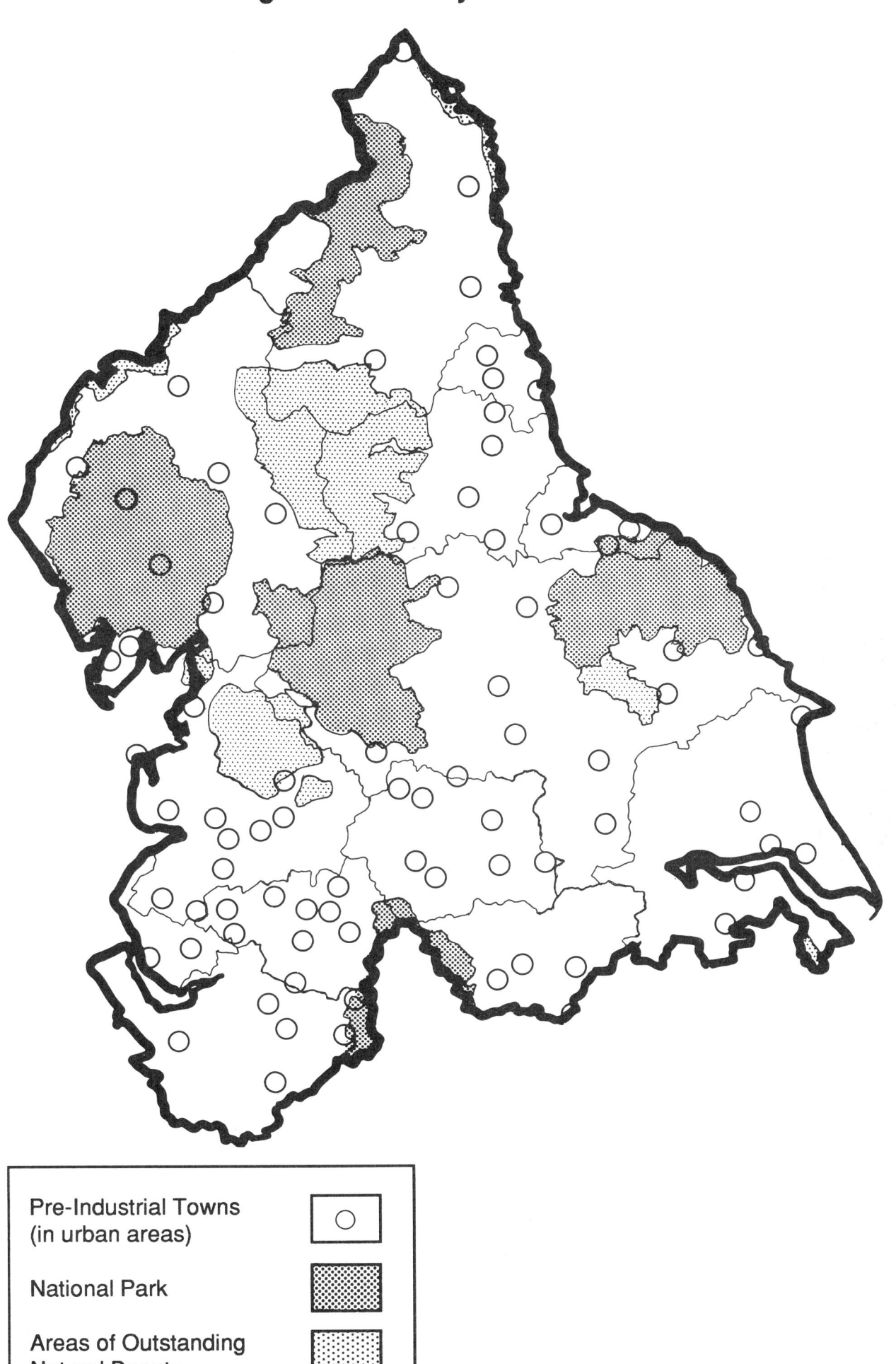

Pre-Industrial Towns (in urban areas)	○
National Park	
Areas of Outstanding Natural Beauty	

TABLE 5
Designated pre-industrial and 19th century towns

	Pre-industrial towns		19th century towns	
	Number	Proportion designated	Number	Proportion designated
Greater Manchester	7	100	60	25
Merseyside	3	100	18	50
South Yorkshire	4	100	22	27
Tyne and Wear	5	60	15	47
West Midlands	8	88	18	50
West Yorkshire	9	89	42	67
Metropolitan Counties	36	89	175	42
Avon	3	67	6	33
Bedfordshire	5	100	4	100
Berkshire	6	100	1	-
Buckinghamshire	8	100	2	-
Cambridgeshire	9	100	4	75
Cheshire	7	100	13	46
Cleveland	4	100	10	70
Cornwall	13	85	8	50
Cumbria	10	100	5	80
Derbyshire	6	100	16	63
Devon	19	95	10	90
Dorset	11	100	3	66
Durham	5	80	9	22
East Sussex	5	80	5	100
Essex	14	100	14	57
Gloucestershire	4	100	3	33
Hampshire	12	100	5	40
Hereford and Worcester	10	90	3	100
Hertfordshire	17	100	5	80
Humberside	7	86	8	63
Isle of Wight	2	100	3	66
Kent	26	88	5	80
Lancashire	11	91	34	38
Leicestershire	7	100	5	40
Lincolnshire	12	100	3	-
Norfolk	13	100	1	100
North Yorkshire	11	91	4	75
Northamptonshire	7	86	7	29
Northumberland	5	80	6	33
Nottinghamshire	7	71	9	44
Oxfordshire	11	100	-	-
Shropshire	3	66	3	33
Somerset	13	100	2	50
Staffordshire	10	90	3	33
Suffolk	17	88	1	100
Surrey	9	100	9	33
Warwickshire	5	100	2	50
West Sussex	6	100	7	86
Wiltshire	12	100	1	100
Shire Counties	362	94	239	54
ENGLAND	398	94	414	49

Figure 4
Town Centres Designated as Conservation Areas

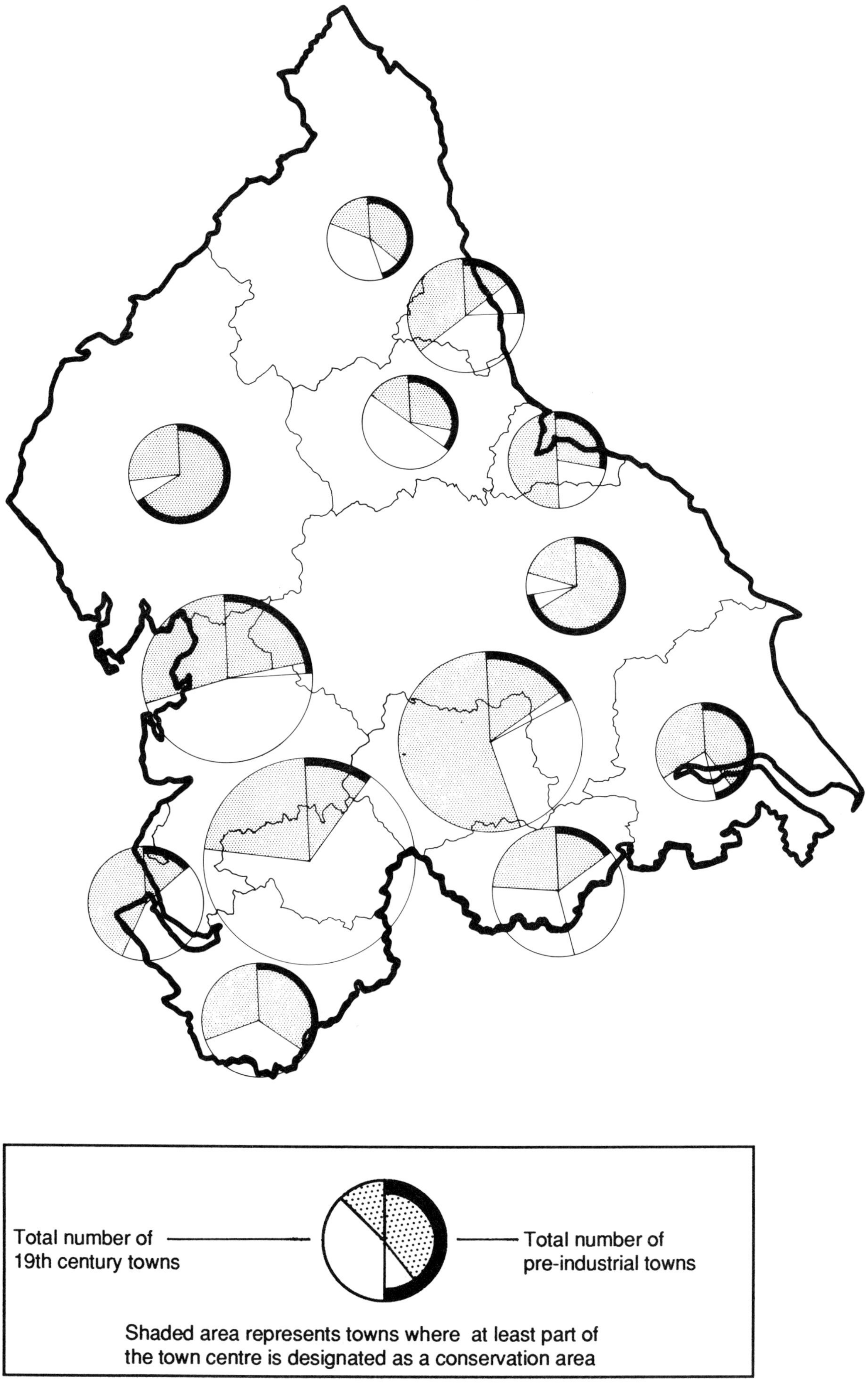

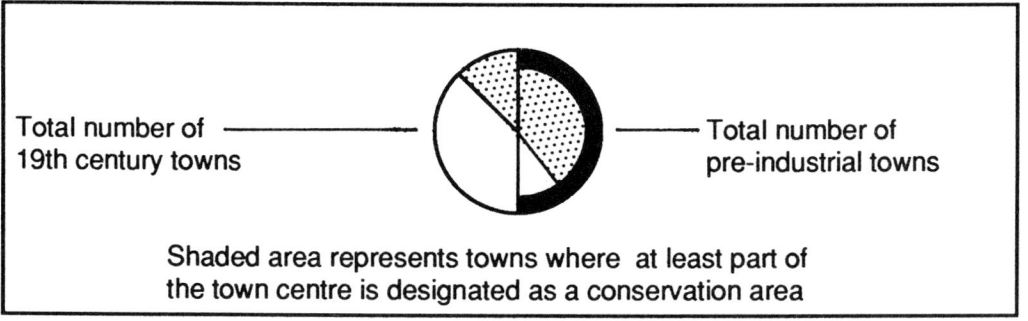

Total number of 19th century towns

Total number of pre-industrial towns

Shaded area represents towns where at least part of the town centre is designated as a conservation area

TABLE 6

Spatial coverage of conservation areas, by type of settlement*

	Towns No	%	Villages No	%	TOTAL No	%
Bulk of settlement	8	0.6	1785	46.4	1793	34.3
Bulk of core	424	30.6	1692	44.0	2116	40.5
Part of core	335	24.2	328	8.5	663	12.7
Large part excluding core	218	15.7	18	0.5	236	4.5
Small part excluding core	400	28.9	22	0.6	422	8.1
TOTAL	1385	100.0	3845	100.0	5230	100.0

*Conservation areas relating to London and urban and rural 'non settlements' are excluded from the table.

TABLE 7

Predominant urban land uses within conservation areas, by type of settlement

	London No	%	Towns No	%	Villages No	%	Non settlements No	%	ENGLAND No	%
Residential	390	79.8	1056	76.2	3743	97.3	33	15.4	5222	88.0
Open space	141	28.8	478	34.5	608	15.8	28	13.1	1255	21.2
Shops/offices	129	26.4	648	46.8	15	0.4	-	-	792	13.3
Industrial	30	6.1	142	10.3	74	1.9	19	8.9	265	4.5
Other	152	31.1	540	39.0	671	17.5	19	8.9	1382	23.3
Total number of conservation areas	489		1385		3845		214		5933	

of the settlement and almost as many again embrace the bulk of the village core. In this instance the 'core' implies not the commercial centre but the whole of the historic or 'pre-1914' village. Thus 90% of village designations broadly include the historic settlement as a whole.

Land uses

The pattern of land uses within conservation areas tells us a good deal about the character of the area. Land use here implies those broad uses which occur within settlements. These are primarily residential, open space, shops/offices and industrial. The term 'other' is used to include smaller groups of shops outside the town centre and in village centres; it also encompasses educational, ecclesiastical and a variety of other uses. Some non-settlement designations also include areas in urban land use, but these are normally ancilliary to a major feature of interest (Table 7).

In towns, nearly half the designations include shops and offices in town centre locations. But only one in ten areas comprise industrial uses. Three quarters of all areas include residential use and a third contain areas of open space. Nearly 40% include 'other' urban land uses. In London the picture is similar but only a quarter of all designations include shops and offices and only about 6% have industrial uses.

Village designations tend to be solely residential; only 3% lack residential uses; 16% include open space in the sense of space for urban parks or specific recreational uses of an urban nature. A similar proportion include 'other' uses such as streets in shopping use or areas in educational, ecclesiastical or other urban use.

In towns, land use information helps to distinguish between those conservation areas which are almost wholly confined to the core (ie town centre), and those which include the whole or part of the core but which extend beyond to embrace older housing areas of historic character or perhaps a Victorian park or industrial area.

National parks and areas of outstanding natural beauty

Given the importance of settlements to the character of areas such as the Cotswolds and the Peak District it is of interest to take stock of the pattern of conservation areas in national parks and areas of outstanding natural beauty. (The distribution of these special areas of countryside within the region covered by this volume is shown in figure 3). There are seven national parks in England and, together with the New Forest, they include 112 conservation areas. The national parks are generally wild and sparsely populated and it is not altogether surprising that the number of designations should be comparatively small (Table 8). However, in such areas thought is now being given to extending urban conservation measures to the protection of built features in the landscape, for example walls and farm buildings.

There are thirty four areas of outstanding natural beauty (AONB's) in England and these contain 766 conservation areas. The number undoubtedly reflects the greater density of rural settlements within AONB's as compared with national parks and the need to afford protection to towns and villages within their landscape settings.

Special features

Where the shape and size of a designated area is affected by the presence of a 'special feature' the

TABLE 8

Conservation areas in national parks and areas of outstanding natural beauty

(a)	National Parks and New Forest	Number of conservation areas
A.	Dartmoor	17
B.	Exmoor	8
C.	Lake District	13
D.	New Forest	10
E.	North Yorkshire	25
F.	Northumberland	-
G.	Peak District	20
H.	Yorkshire Dales	19
TOTAL		112

(b)	Areas of outstanding natural beauty	
1.	Arnside and Silverdale	3
2.	Cannock Chase	4
3.	Chichester Harbour	10
4.	Chilterns	49
5.	Cornwall	28
6.	Cotswolds	94
7.	Cranborne Chase and West Wiltshire Downs	39
8.	Dedham Vale	7
9.	Dorset	42
10.	East Devon	6
11.	East Hampshire	18
12.	Forest of Bowland	15
13.	High Weald	39
14.	Howardian Hills	6
15.	Isles of Scilly	1
16.	Isle of Wight	12
17.	Kent Downs	68
18.	Lincolnshire Wolds	2
19.	Malvern Hills	2
20.	Mendip Hills	4
21.	Norfolk Coast	37
22.	North Devon	10
23.	North Pennines	4
24.	North Wessex Downs	82
25.	Northumberland Coast	3
26.	Quantock Hills	1
27.	Shropshire Hills	9
28.	Solway Coast	6
29.	South Devon	21
30.	South Hampshire Coast	3
31.	Suffolk Coast and Heaths	10
32.	Surrey Hills	36
33.	South Downs	87
34.	Wye Valley	8
TOTAL		766

feature in question is shown in the inventory. Most conservation areas comprise built up areas in various land uses but there are many examples in which the designated areas have been shaped to include a particular feature, or an area of land which is not in normal urban use. In some cases designations are wholly related to a special feature.

Two broad categories of special features are indicated; the first relates to buildings or structures and their associated grounds; the second to topographical features. In all, some 8,800 special features have been identified, 45% being associated with built and 55% with topographical features. (Table 9)

Taking built features first, we find that agricultural buildings, which largely comprise farmsteads and mills, and buildings in residential use, for example country and town houses, jointly account for over 68% of all built features. Of the remaining categories, 11% include industrial buildings, transport and engineering structures, for example bridges, mills, canals and dockyard buildings. Archaeological, defensive and ecclesiastical features each account for about 5% of the total; the most common features here being medieval earthworks, redundant abbeys and priories, and castles and forts.

Amongst the topographical categories it is clear that water features -mostly rivers but also ponds - dominate, accounting for over 40% of the total. In addition we find that over a third of topographical features comprise cultivated land, for example farmland and meadows, or open country, including woodland, commons etc. A substantial proportion of designations are also influenced by the presence of private parkland normally associated with major houses. Coastal features and locations are another significant category.

An investigation of the pattern of special features within conservation areas in different types of settlement reveals, perhaps not surprisingly, that the number of special features, proportionately at least, is greatest in the case of the 214 'non-settlements'. These are, by definition, associated with isolated built or topographical features. Notable here are the high number of water and industrial and transport features, particularly rivers and canals.

TABLE 9

Special features in conservation areas by type of settlement

	London	Towns	Villages	Non settlements	ENGLAND
(a) Built features					
Agricultural	2	75	1261	69	1407
Residential	28	122	1087	65	1302
Industrial/Transport	10	166	199	69	444
Archaeological	3	14	234	16	267
Defensive	3	108	119	16	246
Ecclesiastical	9	73	84	19	185
Civic/Institutional	16	33	67	3	119
Sub-Total	**71**	**591**	**3051**	**257**	**3970**
(b) Topographical features					
Water	52	333	1507	94	1986
Cultivated land	-	58	843	41	942
Parkland	30	82	630	52	794
Open country	27	74	653	38	792
Coastal	-	162	121	19	302
Leisure/tourism	1	4	7	2	14
Sub-Total	**110**	**713**	**3761**	**246**	**4830**
TOTAL	**181**	**1304**	**6812**	**503**	**8800**

NOTES

The main components in the above groups are as follows:-

(a) **Built features**

Agricultural	:	farmsteads (980), water mills (373)
Residential	:	major town and country houses in grounds (1255)
Industrial/Transport	:	canals/locks (156), bridges/fords (113)
Archaeological	:	moated sites (120)
Defensive	:	castles/forts (198)
Ecclesiastical	:	monastic houses (104)
Civic/Institutional	:	almshouses (65)

(b) **Topographical features**

Water	:	rivers and streams (1669), ponds (300)
Open country	:	commons and greens (417), woodland (293)
Coastal	:	seafronts (145)

GREATER MANCHESTER

Bolton

1. BOLTON, BANK TOP
   1970
   Town (147), Pre-industrial Town
   Large Part Excluding Core
   Residential

2. BOLTON, BARROWBRIDGE
   1970
   Town (147), Pre-industrial Town
   Small Part Excluding Core
   Residential, Open Space

3. BOLTON, BIRLEY STREET
   1970
   Town (147), Pre-industrial Town
   Small Part Excluding Core
   Residential, Other

4. BOLTON, CHORLEY NEW ROAD
   1974
   Town (147), Pre-industrial Town
   Large Part Excluding Core
   Residential, Open Space

5. BOLTON, CHURCHGATE
   1970
   Town (147), Pre-industrial Town
   Including Part of Core
   Shops/Offices, Other

6. BOLTON, DEANE VILLAGE
   1970
   Town (147), Pre-industrial Town
   Small Part Excluding Core
   Residential, Open Space, Other

7. BOLTON, EAGLEY BANK
   1975 (1970) Amended
   Town (147), Pre-industrial Town
   Small Part Excluding Core
   Residential, Open Space, Industrial
   Country House

8. BOLTON, FIRWOOD FOLD
   1969
   Urban Non Settlement (147)
   Not Applicable
   Reservoir, River

9. BOLTON, HILL TOP
   1975 (1970) Amended
   Urban Non Settlement (147)
   Not Applicable
   Residential, Open Space
   Reservoir

10. BOLTON, MAWDSLEY STREET / NELSON SQUARE
    1970
    Town (147), Pre-industrial Town
    Including Part of Core
    Shops/Offices

11. BOLTON, SILVERWELL STREET / WOOD STREET
    1970
    Town (147), Pre-industrial Town
    Including Part of Core
    Shops/Offices

12. BOLTON, ST. PAULS HALLIWELL
    1975 (1970) Amended
    Town (147), Pre-industrial Town
    Small Part Excluding Core
    Residential, Open Space, Other

13. BRADSHAW CHAPEL
    1976
    Urban Village (22)
    Bulk of Settlement
    Residential, Open Space, Other
    Reservoir, River

14. DUNSCAR FOLD
    1983
    Urban Non-Settlement (22)
    Not Applicable
    Farmstead, Reservoir, River

15. EGERTON
    1980
    Urban Village (22)
    Including Bulk of Core
    Residential, Open Space, Other

16. FARNWORTH, GREENSIDE
    1975
    Town (25)
    Small Part Excluding Core
    Residential

17. RIDING GATE
    1976
    Urban Village (22)
    Bulk of Settlement
    Residential
    Moorland, Farmsteads

18. WALLSUCHES (NR. HORWICH)
    1975
    Urban Village (18)
    Bulk of Settlement
    Residential, Open Space, Industrial
    Moorland, Reservoirs, Woodland,
    Farmsteads, Stream

19. WESTHOUGHTON
    1980
    Town (21)
    Including Bulk of Core
    Residential, Shops/Offices, Other

Bury

1. AINSWORTH (NR. RADCLIFFE)
   1973
   Urban Village (31)
   Including Bulk of Core
   Residential, Open Space

2. BROOKSBOTTOM / ROWLANDS
   1975
   Urban Village (18)
   Bulk of Settlement
   Residential, Open Space, Industrial
   River

3. BURY, TOWN CENTRE
   1978
   Town (68)
   Including Bulk of Core
   Shops/Offices, Other

4. HOLCOMBE (NR. RAMSBOTTOM)
   1978 (1970) Amended
   Urban Village (15)
   Bulk of Settlement
   Residential, Open Space
   Farmland, Moorland, Woodland,
   Farmstead, .Country
   House(Sanatorium)

5. HOLCOMBE, POT GREEN
   1976
   Urban Village (15)
   Including Bulk of Core
   Residential, Open Space
   Stream, Green

6. MOUNT PLEASANT (NR. BURY)
   1974
   Urban Non Settlement (68)
   Not Applicable
   Residential, Industrial
   Industrial Mill

7. RAMSBOTTOM, TOWN CENTRE
   1977
   Town (15)
   Including Bulk of Core
   Shops/Offices

GREATER MANCHESTER

8. SUMMERSEAT
   (NR. RAMSBOTTOM)
   1975
   Urban Village (15)
   Including Bulk of Core
   Residential, Open Space
   Country House, Park, River

Manchester

1. ALBERT SQUARE
   1985 (1972) Amended
   Town (449), Pre-industrial Town
   Including Part of Core
   Open Space, Shops/Offices
   Town Hall

2. BLACKBURN PARK
   1980
   Town (449), Pre-industrial Town
   Large Part Excluding Core
   Residential

3. CASTLEFIELD
   1985 (1979) Amended
   Town (449), Pre-industrial Town
   Including Part of Core
   Industrial, Other
   Industrial Monument(Railway
   Station/Depot/Warehouses), Canal,
   Rivers, Roman Fort

4. CATHEDRAL
   1972
   Town (449), Pre-industrial Town
   Including Part of Core
   Shops/Offices, Other
   Cathedral, River, School

5. CHORLTON GREEN
   1970
   Town (449), Pre-industrial Town
   Small Part Excluding Core
   Residential, Open Space, Other

6. CRAB LANE, BLACKLEY
   1983
   Town (449), Pre-industrial Town
   Small Part Excluding Core
   Residential, Open Space

7. DEANSGATE / PETER STREET
   1985
   Town (449), Pre-industrial Town
   Including Part of Core
   Shops/Offices

8. DIDSBURY ST. JAMES
   1970
   Town (449), Pre-industrial Town
   Small Part Excluding Core
   Residential, Open Space, Other
   River

9. GEORGE STREET
   1985
   Town (449), Pre-industrial Town
   Including Part of Core
   Shops/Offices
   River

10. NORTHENDEN
    1981
    Town (449), Pre-industrial Town
    Small Part Excluding Core
    Residential, Other
    River

11. PARSONAGE GARDENS
    1985
    Town (449) Pre-Industrial Town
    Including Part of Core
    Shops/Offices
    River

12. RUSHFORD PARK VILLAGE
    1986
    Town (449), Pre-industrial Town
    Small Part Excluding Core
    Residential

13. ST. ANNS SQUARE
    1970
    Town (449), Pre-industrial Town
    Including Part of Core
    Shops/Offices, Other

14. ST. JOHN STREET
    1970
    Town (449), Pre-industrial Town
    Including Part of Core
    Open Space, Shops/Offices

15. ST. PETERS SQUARE
    1974
    Town (449), Pre-industrial Town
    Including Part of Core
    Open Space, Shops/Offices

16. UPPER KING STREET
    1985 (1970) Amended
    Town (449), Pre-industrial Town
    Including Part of Core
    Shops/Offices

17. VICTORIA PARK
    1972
    Town (449),
    Large Part Excluding Core
    Residential, Open Space

18. WHITWORTH STREET
    1985 (1974) Amended
    Town (449), Pre-industrial Town
    Including Part of Core
    Shops/Offices

19. WITHINGTON
    1983
    Town (449), Pre-industrial Town
    Small Part Excluding Core
    Residential, Other

Oldham

1. BOARSHURST
   (NR. UPPERMILL)
   1975
   Urban Village (22)
   Bulk of Settlement
   Residential

2. BOTTOM OF WOODHOUSES
   (NR. FAILSWORTH)
   1979
   Urban Non Settlement (22)
   Not Applicable
   Residential

3. DELPH (NR. UPPERMILL)
   1973
   Urban Village (22)
   Bulk of Settlement
   Residential, Industrial
   Industrial Mills, River

4. DELPH, GRANGE HAMLET
   (NR.UPPERMILL)
   1982
   Urban Non-Settlement (22)
   Not Applicable
   Farmstead

5. DELPH, NEW TAME
   (NR.UPPERMILL)
   1980
   Urban Non Settlement (22)
   Not Applicable
   Farmstead

6. DIGLEA (NR. UPPERMILL)
   1972
   Urban Village (22)
   Bulk of Settlement
   Residential

7. DOBCROSS (NR. UPPERMILL)
   1972
   Urban Village (22)
   Including Bulk of Core
   Residential, Other

8. GRASSCROFT (NR. UPPERMILL)
   1974
   Urban Village (22)
   Including Bulk of Core
   Residential

GREATER MANCHESTER

9. HARROP GREEN
   (NR. UPPERMILL)
   1972
   Urban Village (22)
   Bulk of Settlement
   Residential

10. LEES
    1975
    Town (5)
    Including Bulk of Core
    Residential, Shops/Offices,
    Industrial

11. LYDGATE (NR. UPPERMILL)
    1983
    Urban Village (22)
    Bulk of Settlement
    Residential, Other

12. OLDHAM, ALEXANDRA PARK
    1976
    Town (95)
    Large Part Excluding Core
    Residential, Open Space

13. OLDHAM, TOWN CENTRE
    1975
    Town (95)
    Including Bulk of Core
    Shops/Offices, Other

14. ROYAL GEORGE MILLS,
    FRIEZLAND (NR. UPPERMILL)
    1982
    Urban Non-Settlement (22)
    Not Applicable
    Industrial
    Industrial Mills, Canal, River,
    Reservoir

15. SCOUTHEAD (NR. UPPERMILL)
    1975
    Urban Village (22)
    Bulk of Settlement
    Residential

16. UPPERMILL
    1977
    Town (22)
    Including Bulk of Core
    Residential, Shops/Offices,
    Industrial
    Canal, River, Mill

17. WOODHOUSES
    (NR. FAILSWORTH)
    1975
    Urban Village (22)
    Bulk of Settlement
    Residential

Rochdale

1. ASHWORTH FOLD
   (NR. HEYWOOD)
   1974
   Urban Non Settlement (31)
   Not Applicable
   Farmstead

2. HIGHER AND LOWER OGDEN
   (NR. MILNROW)
   1974
   Urban Non Settlement (12)
   Not Applicable
   Residential

3. HOLLINGWORTH FOLD
   (NR.LITTLEBOROUGH)
   1982
   Urban Village (14)
   Bulk of Settlement
   Residential

4. LITTLEBOROUGH,
   TOWN CENTRE
   1977
   Town (14)
   Including Bulk of Core
   Residential, Shops/Offices

5. MIDDLETON, TOWN CENTRE
   1978
   Town (52)
   Including Bulk of Core
   Shops/Offices, Other

6. MILNROW, CLEGG VILLAGE
   1986
   Urban Non-Settlement (12)
   Not Applicable
   Industrial
   Industrial Mills, Canal, Reservoir

7. RAKEWOOD
   (NR.LITTLEBOROUGH)
   1982
   Urban Non-Settlement (14)
   Not Applicable
   Industrial
   Industrial Mills

8. ROCHDALE, TOAD LANE
   1977
   Town (93), Pre-industrial Town
   Including Part of Core
   Shops/Offices, Other

9. ROCHDALE, TOWN CENTRE
   1980
   Town (93), Pre-industrial Town
   Including Bulk of Core
   Open Space, Shops/Offices, Other

10. WARDLE
    1974
    Town (7)
    Including Bulk of Core
    Residential, Other

11. WHITTAKER
    (NR.LITTLEBOROUGH)
    1982
    Urban Village (14)
    Bulk of Settlement
    Residential

Salford

1. ECCLES,
   BARTON UPON IRWELL
   1976
   Town (37)
   Large Part Excluding Core
   Residential, Other
   Canal, Farmland

2. ECCLES, MONTON GREEN
   1979
   Town (37)
   Small Part Excluding Core
   Open Space, Other

3. PENDLEBURY,
   ST. AUGUSTINES
   1977
   Town (40)
   Small Part Excluding Core
   Other

4. ROE GREEN / BEESLEY GREEN
   1970
   Urban Village (49)
   Including Bulk of Core
   Residential, Open Space

5. SALFORD, SACRED TRINITY /
   FLAT IRON
   1978
   Town (98), Pre-industrial Town
   Including Part of Core
   Shops/Offices, Other

6. SALFORD, THE ADELPHI /
   BEXLEY SQUARE
   1978
   Town (98), Pre-industrial Town
   Including Bulk of Core
   Shops/Offices, Other

7. SALFORD, THE CLIFF
   1976
   Town (98), Pre-industrial Town
   Large Part Excluding Core
   Residential
   River

GREATER MANCHESTER

8. SALFORD, THE CRESCENT
   1981
   Town (98), Pre-industrial Town
   Including Part of Core
   Other
   River

9. WORSLEY
   1969
   Twin Town (49)
   Large Part Excluding Core
   Other

10. WORSLEY OLD HALL
    1982
    Urban Non-Settlement (49)
    Not Applicable
    Other
    Country House, Farmstead

11. WORSLEY, ST. MARKS
    1981
    Twin Town (49)
    Small Part Excluding Core
    Other

Stockport

1. BROOKBOTTOM (NR. MARPLE)
   1976
   Urban Non Settlement (24)
   Not Applicable
   Farmland, Stream, Woodland,
   Farmstead, River

2. CHEADLE HULME NUCLEUS,
   HULME HALL ROAD ETC
   1984
   Town (59)
   Including Bulk of Core
   Residential, Other

3. CHEADLE, TOWN CENTRE
   1974
   Town (59)
   Including Bulk of Core
   Residential, Shops/Offices, Other

4. CHEADLE-GATLEY,
   BROOKLYN CRESCENT
   1980
   Town (59)
   Large Part Excluding Core
   Residential

5. CHEADLE-GATLEY,
   GATLEY GREEN
   1980
   Town (59)
   Including Bulk of Core
   Residential, Open Space, Shops/
   Offices, Other

6. COMPSTALL (NR. BREDBURY-
   ROMILEY)
   1974
   Urban Village (29)
   Including Bulk of Core
   Residential, Industrial, Other

7. MARPLE BRIDGE,
   (NR. MARPLE)
   1974
   Urban Village (24)
   Including Bulk of Core
   Residential, Other
   Woodland, River, Bridge

8. MELLOR, MILL BROW
   (NR. MARPLE)
   1978
   Urban Village (24)
   Bulk of Settlement
   Residential
   Woodland, Farmland, Stream

9. MELLOR, MOOR END
   (NR. MARPLE)
   1978
   Urban Village (24)
   Bulk of Settlement
   Residential
   Farmland, Stream

10. STOCKPORT,
    DAVENPORT PARK
    1980
    Town (136), Pre-industrial Town
    Small Part Excluding Core
    Residential

11. STOCKPORT, DODGE HILL
    1985
    Town (136), Pre-industrial Town
    Small Part Excluding Core
    Other
    Town House

12. STOCKPORT,
    HEATON MERSEY
    1978
    Town (136), Pre-industrial Town
    Small Part Excluding Core
    Residential, Open Space, Other

13. STOCKPORT, HEATON MOOR
    ROAD / MAULDETH ROAD
    1986 (1973) Amended
    Town (136), Pre-industrial Town
    Large Part Excluding Core
    Residential, Other

14. STOCKPORT, MARKET PLACE /
    UNDERBANKS
    1974
    Town (136), Pre-industrial Town
    Including Bulk of Core
    Shops/Offices

Tameside

1. ASHTON-UNDER-LYNE,
   TOWN CENTRE
   1979
   Town (45)
   Including Bulk of Core
   Shops/Offices

2. CARRBROOK (NR. MOSSLEY)
   1976
   Urban Village (10)
   Including Bulk of Core
   Residential, Industrial

3. DROYLESDEN, FAIRFIELD
   1976 (1971) Amended
   Town (23)
   Small Part Excluding Core
   Residential, Open Space
   Planned community

4. MOTTRAM IN LONGDENDALE
   1985 (1973) Amended
   Twin Town (11)
   Including Bulk of Core
   Residential, Shops/Offices
   Farmland

5. STALYBRIDGE, COPLEY,
   ST. PAULS
   1986
   Town (26)
   Small Part Excluding Core
   Industrial, Other
   Industrial Mill

Trafford

1. ALTRINCHAM, GOOSE GREEN
   1973
   Town (40), Pre-industrial Town
   Including Part of Core
   Residential, Open Space

2. ALTRINCHAM, LINOTYPE
   HOUSING ESTATE
   1985
   Town (40), Pre-industrial Town
   Small Part Excluding Core
   Residential

GREATER MANCHESTER

3. ALTRINCHAM, OLD MARKET PLACE
1986 (1973) Amended
Town (40), Pre-industrial Town
Including Bulk of Core
Shops/Offices

4. ALTRINCHAM, SANDIWAY
1975
Town (40), Pre-industrial Town
Large Part Excluding Core
Residential, Other

5. BOWDON
1974 (1973) Amended
Town (5)
Including Bulk of Core
Residential, Shops/Offices, Other

6. BOWDON, ASHLEY HEATH
1974
Town (5)
Large Part Excluding Core
Residential, Open Space

7. BOWDON, DEVISDALE
1974
Town (5)
Large Part Excluding Core
Residential, Open Space

8. BOWDON, THE DOWNS
1974 (1973) Amended
Town (5)
Large Part Excluding Core
Residential

9. DUNHAM TOWN
1975
Rural Other Settlement
Including Bulk of Core
Residential
Farmland

10. DUNHAM WOODHOUSES
1975
Rural Other Settlement
Bulk of Settlement
Residential

11. SALE, ASHTON ON MERSEY
1976
Town (58)
Small Part Excluding Core
Residential, Other
Farmland

12. SALE, BROGDEN GROVE
1976
Town (58)
Small Part Excluding Core
Residential

13. SOUTH HALE
1986
Town (16)
Large Part Excluding Core
Residential

14. URMSTON, FLIXTON
1975
Town (44)
Small Part Excluding Core
Residential

15. WARBURTON
1975
Rural Main Settlement
Bulk of Settlement
Residential

Wigan

1. HAIGH
1976
Rural Main Settlement
Bulk of Settlement
Residential, Open Space, Other
Farmland, Cemetary

2. LEIGH, MARKET STREET
1981
Town (45)
Including Part of Core
Shops/Offices, Other

3. STANDISH
1976
Town (12)
Including Part of Core
Shops/Offices, Other

4. WIGAN, DICCONSON
1982
Town (80), Pre-industrial Town
Including Part of Core
Residential, Other

5. WIGAN, MESNES PARK
1984 (1980) Amended
Town (80), Pre-industrial Town
Large Part Excluding Core
Residential, Open Space, Industrial, Other

6. WIGAN, TOWN CENTRE
1984 (1980) Amended
Town (80), Pre-industrial Town
Including Bulk of Core
Shops/Offices, Other

DESIGNATION ACTIVITY 1987

Bolton

20	BOLTON, TOWN CENTRE	
21	HORWICH, TOWN CENTRE	
5	BOLTON, CHURCHGATE	(EXTENSION)

Manchester

20	SHUDEHILL
21	SMITHFIELD
22	STEVENSON SQUARE

GREATER MANCHESTER

Salford 1 ECCLES, BARTON UPON IRWELL (EXTENSION)
3 PENBLEBURY, ST AUGUSTINES (EXTENSION)

Stockport 15 DAVENPORT, THE CRESCENT/EGERTON ROAD

Trafford 16 ALTRINCHAM, GEORGE STREET
17 ALTRINCHAM, STAMFORD NEW ROAD
6 BOWDON, ASHLEY HEATH (EXTENSION)

Wigan 7 WIGAN PIER
8 ATHERTON, HOWE BRIDGE

DESIGNATION ACTIVITY 1988

Bury 7 RAMSBOTTOM (EXTENSION)

Manchester 23 WEST DIDSBURY, ALBERT PARK
22 STEVENSON SQUARE (EXTENSION)

Stockport 16 MARPLE, STATION ROAD/WINNINGTON ROAD
14 MARKET PLACE, UNDERBANKS (EXTENSION)

Trafford 18 HALE, STATION
8 BOWDEN, THE DOWNS (EXTENSION)

Wigan 9 SHEVINGTON, CHURCH LANE
3 STANDISH (EXTENSION)
4 WIGAN, DICCONSON (EXTENSION)
6 WIGAN, TOWN CENTRE (EXTENSION)

FOOTNOTES

Manchester

4. CATHEDRAL   This Conservation Area extends into Salford, GREATER MANCHESTER.

Salford

1. ECCLES, BARTON-UPON-IRWELL   This Conservation Area extends into Trafford, GREATER MANCHESTER.

Stockport

1. BROOKBOTTOM (NR MARPLE) This Conservation Area extends into High Peak, DERBYSHIRE.

GREATER MANCHESTER

FOOTNOTES continued ...

4. CHEADLE-GATLEY,
   BROOKLYN CRESCENT   The town has three historic nuclei, Cheadle, Cheadle Hulme and Gatley. Details as to scale of coverage which relate to the core refer to the relevant nucleus.

13. STOCKPORT, HEATON
    MOOR RD / MAULDETH RD   Original designation of 1973 cancelled in 1974.

FOOTNOTES continued ...

MERSEYSIDE

Knowsley

1. CRONTON, TOWN END
   1978
   Rural Main Settlement
   Including Part of Core
   Residential, Other

2. HALEWOOD VILLAGE
   1978
   Rural Main Settlement
   Including Bulk of Core
   Residential

3. HUYTON-ROBY, HUYTON CHURCH
   1978
   Town (58)
   Including Part of Core
   Residential, Other

4. HUYTON-ROBY, THE ORCHARD
   1978
   Town (58)
   Small Part Excluding Core
   Other
   Country House, Park

5. HUYTON-ROBY, VICTORIA / CHURCH ROAD
   1978
   Town (58)
   Small Part Excluding Core
   Residential

6. HUYTON-ROBY, ROBY NUCLEUS
   1978
   Town (58)
   Including Bulk of Core
   Residential

7. INGOE LANE (NR.KIRKBY)
   1978
   Urban Non Settlement (51)
   Not Applicable
   Residential, Other

8. KIRKBY, OLD HALL LANE
   1978
   Town (51)
   Small Part Excluding Core
   Open Space, Other

9. KNOWSLEY VILLAGE
   1978
   Rural Main Settlement
   Including Bulk of Core
   Residential, Open Space
   Country House, Farmsteads

10. PRESCOT, TOWN CENTRE
    1979 (1974) Amended
    Town (11), Pre-industrial Town
    Including Bulk of Core
    Residential, Shops/Offices

11. TARBOCK GREEN
    1978
    Rural Other Settlement
    Bulk of Settlement
    Residential
    Stream

12. TARBOCK VILLAGE
    1978
    Rural Main Settlement
    Bulk of Settlement
    Residential
    Farmstead

Liverpool

1. ALBERT DOCK
   1977
   Urban Non Settlement (510),
   Pre-industrial Town
   Not Applicable
   Industrial Monument (Docks), River Estuary

2. CANNING STREET
   1977 (1972) Amended
   Town (510), Pre-industrial Town
   Small Part Excluding Core
   Residential

3. CASTLE STREET
   1985 (1968) Amended
   Town (510), Pre-industrial Town
   Including Part of Core
   Shops/Offices

4. CHILDWALL ABBEY
   1969
   Town (510), Pre-industrial Town
   Small Part Excluding Core
   Other

5. DERWENT SQUARE
   1981
   Town (510), Pre-industrial Town
   Small Part Excluding Core
   Residential

6. EDGE HILL
   1979
   Town (510), Pre-industrial Town
   Small Part Excluding Core
   Residential

7. FULWOOD PARK
   1973
   Town (510), Pre-industrial Town
   Small Part Excluding Core
   Residential
   River Estuary

8. GATEACRE VILLAGE
   1982 (1969) Amended
   Town (510), Pre-industrial Town
   Small Part Excluding Core
   Residential, Other

9. GRASSENDALE / CRESSINGTON PARK
   1968
   Town (510)
   Small Part Excluding Core
   Open Space
   River Estuary

10. GROVE PARK
    1977
    Town (510), Pre-industrial Town
    Small Part Excluding Core
    Residential

11. HUNTS CROSS AVENUE
    1971
    Town (510), Pre-industrial Town
    Large Part Excluding Core
    Residential

12. LARK LANE
    1976
    Town (510), Pre-industrial Town
    Small Part Excluding Core
    Residential, Other

13. MILL BANK
    1971
    Town (510), Pre-industrial Town
    Small Part Excluding Core
    Residential

14. MOSSLEY HILL
    1985 (1971) Amended
    Town (510), Pre-industrial Town
    Large Part Excluding Core
    Residential, Open Space, Other

15. MOUNT PLEASANT
    1976
    Town (510), Pre-industrial Town
    Part of Core
    Other
    Cathedral

16. MUIRHEAD AVENUE
    1971
    Town (510), Pre-industrial Town
    Large Part Excluding Core
    Residential

MERSEYSIDE

17. NEWENHAM CRESCENT
   1972
   Town (510), Pre-industrial Town
   Large Part Excluding Core
   Residential

18. NEWSHAM PARK
   1982
   Town (510), Pre-industrial Town
   Small Part Excluding Core
   Residential, Open Space

19. OGDEN CLOSE
   1971
   Town (510), Pre-industrial Town
   Small Part Excluding Core
   Residential

20. PRINCES PARK
   1971
   Town (510), Pre-industrial Town
   Large Part Excluding Core
   Residential, Open Space

21. PRINCES ROAD
   1972
   Town (510), Pre-industrial Town
   Small Part Excluding Core
   Residential, Open Space

22. RODNEY STREET
   1977 (1968) Amended
   Town (510), Pre-industrial Town
   Including Part of Core
   Shops/Offices
   Cathedral Precinct

23. SEFTON PARK
   1983 (1971) Amended
   Town (510), Pre-industrial Town
   Large Part Excluding Core
   Residential, Open Space

24. ST. MICHAELS HAMLET
   1969
   Town (510), Pre-industrial Town
   Small Part Excluding Core
   Residential

25. WALTON ON THE HILL
   1977
   Town (510), Pre-industrial Town
   Small Part Excluding Core
   Residential, Other

26. WAVERTREE GARDEN-
   SUBURB
   1972
   Town (510), Pre-industrial Town
   Small Part Excluding Core
   Residential
   Planned community

27. WAVERTREE VILLAGE
   1979
   Town (510), Pre-industrial Town
   Small Part Excluding Core
   Residential, Other

28. WEST DERBY VILLAGE
   1969
   Town (510), Pre-industrial Town
   Small Part Excluding Core
   Residential, Other

29. WILLIAM BROWN STREET
   1969
   Town (510), Pre-industrial Town
   Including Part of Core
   Shops/Offices, Other

30. WOOLTON VILLAGE
   1982 (1970) Amended
   Town (510), Pre-industrial Town
   Small Part Excluding Core
   Residential, Other

St Helens

1. NEWTON LE WILLOWS, HIGH
   STREET
   1977
   Town (20), Pre-industrial Town
   Including Bulk of Core
   Shops/Offices

2. NEWTON LE WILLOWS,
   WILLOW PARK
   1976
   Town (20), Pre-industrial Town
   Including Part of Core
   Open Space
   Castle Mound, Lake

3. RAINFORD
   1977
   Town (9)
   Including Bulk of Core
   Residential

4. RAINHILL
   1976
   Rural Main Settlement
   Including Part of Core
   Residential, Other

5. ST. HELENS, VICTORIA
   SQUARE
   1976
   Town (99)
   Including Part of Core
   Shops/Offices

Sefton

1. CROSBY HALL (NR.CROSBY)
   1985
   Urban Non-Settlement (54)
   Not Applicable
   Country House, Park

2. CROSBY, BLUNDELLSANDS
   PARK
   1983
   Town (54)
   Large Part Excluding Core
   Residential, Open Space

3. CROSBY, WATERLOO
   1972
   Town (54)
   Small Part Excluding Core
   Residential

4. FORMBY, GREEN LANE
   1984
   Town (26)
   Small Part Excluding Core
   Open Space, Other

5. INCE BLUNDELL PARK
   1981
   Rural Non-Settlement
   Not Applicable
   Other
   Country House, Park, Wood

6. LITTLE CROSBY (NR. CROSBY)
   1974
   Urban Village (54)
   Bulk of Settlement
   Residential
   Woodland

7. SEFTON VILLAGE
   1974
   Rural Main Settlement
   Bulk of Settlement
   Residential, Other
   Park, Farmstead, Mill

8. SOUTHPORT, BIRKDALE
   VILLAGE
   1982
   Town (90)
   Small Part Excluding Core
   Residential, Other

9. SOUTHPORT, CHURCHTOWN
   1974
   Town (90)
   Small Part Excluding Core
   Residential, Other

MERSEYSIDE

10. SOUTHPORT, LORD STREET
1973
Town (90)
Including Bulk of Core
Residential, Shops/Offices

Wirral

1. BARNSTON VILLAGE
(NR.HESWALL)
1984
Urban Village (28)
Bulk of Settlement
Residential, Other
Farmstead

2. BEBINGTON, PORT SUNLIGHT
1978
Twin Town (64)
Small Part Excluding Core
Residential
Planned community

3. BIDSTON VILLAGE
(NR. BIRKENHEAD)
1971
Urban Village (124)
Including Bulk of Core
Residential
Country House, Park, Farmsteads

4. BIRKENHEAD, BIRKENHEAD PARK
1977
Town (124)
Large Part Excluding Core
Residential, Open Space

5. BIRKENHEAD, HAMILTON SQUARE
1977
Town (124)
Including Part of Core
Open Space, Shops/Offices

6. BIRKENHEAD, OXTON VILLAGE
1979
Town (124)
Small Part Excluding Core
Residential

7. BIRKENHEAD, ROCK PARK / ROCK FERRY
1979
Town (124)
Small Part Excluding Core
Residential
River Estuary

8. BROMBOROUGH
1982
Twin Town (64)
Including Part of Core
Shops/Offices

9. EASTHAM
(NR. BROMBOROUGH)
1974
Urban Village (64)
Bulk of Settlement
Residential, Open Space
Woodland

10. FRANKBY VILLAGE
(NR. WEST KIRBY)
1974
Urban Village (33)
Bulk of Settlement
Residential
Farmsteads

11. HESWALL, GAYTON
1979
Town (28)
Small Part Excluding Core
Residential
Country House, Park

12. HESWALL, LOWER VILLAGE
1979
Town (28)
Small Part Excluding Core
Residential

13. THORNTON HOUGH
(NR.BEBINGTON)
1974
Urban Village (64)
Including Bulk of Core
Residential, Open Space
Country House

14. THURSTASTON VILLAGE
(NR.HESWALL)
1981
Urban Village (28)
Bulk of Settlement
Residential
Country House, Park, Farmstead,
Woodland

15. WALLASEY, SAUGHALL MASSIE
1973
Town (90)
Small Part Excluding Core
Residential
Farmland

16. WALLASEY, WELLINGTON ROAD
1974
Town (90)
Including Part of Core
Residential, Open Space
Seafront

17. WEST KIRBY
1974
Twin Town (33)
Including Part of Core
Residential, Other

18. WEST KIRBY, CALDY VILLAGE
1985 (1974) Amended
Twin Town (33)
Large Part Excluding Core
Residential

MERSEYSIDE

DESIGNATION ACTIVITY 1987

St Helens   6   NEWTON-LE-WILLOWS, VULCAN VILLAGE

Sefton   11   CROSBY, MOOR PARK

Wirral   19   BROMBOROUGH ROAD

DESIGNATION ACTIVITY 1988

Liverpool   31   SHAW STREET
                 32   DUKE SREET

Sefton   12   SOUTHPORT, WEST BIRKDALE
               13   SOUTHPORT, NORTH MEOLS

FOOTNOTES

Knowsley

3. HUYTON-ROBY, HUYTON CHURCH   The town has two nuclei, Huyton and Roby. Details as to scale of coverage which relate to the core refer to the relevant nucleus.

SOUTH YORKSHIRE

SOUTH YORKSHIRE

Barnsley

1. BARNSLEY, CHURCH /
REGENT STREET
1977 (1974) Amended
Town (74)
Including Bulk of Core
Shops/Offices

2. BARNSLEY, HUDDERSFIELD
ROAD / SALISBURY STREET
1974
Town (74)
Large Part Excluding Core
Residential

3. BARNSLEY, HUDDERSFIELD
ROAD / VICTORIA ROAD
1979 (1975) Amended
Town (74)
Large Part Excluding Core
Residential

4. BILLINGLEY
1974
Rural Main Settlement
Bulk of Settlement
Residential
Farmsteads

5. CARLTON (NR. BARNSLEY)
1977
Urban Village (74)
Including Bulk of Core
Residential

6. CAWTHORNE
1979 (1971) Amended
Rural Main Settlement
Bulk of Settlement
Residential
Stream

7. DARFIELD
1980
Town (8)
Including Bulk of Core
Residential, Other

8. HIGH HOYLAND
1974
Rural Main Settlement
Bulk of Settlement
Residential
Farmstead

9. HOYLAND NETHER, ELSECAR
1974
Town (15)
Large Part Excluding Core
Residential, Industrial, Other
Canal

10. HOYLANDSWAINE
(NR. PENISTONE)
1978
Urban Village (9)
Bulk of Settlement
Residential
Farmstead

11. INGBIRCHWORTH
1974
Rural Other Settlement
Bulk of Settlement
Residential, Open Space
River

12. LANGSETT
1977
Rural Main Settlement
Bulk of Settlement
Residential
National Park(G)
Country House

13. PENISTONE
1980 (1974) Amended
Town (9)
Including Bulk of Core
Residential, Shops/Offices

14. THURLSTONE (NR.PENISTONE)
1974
Urban Village (9)
Including Bulk of Core
Residential, Other
River, Country House

15. WORSBROUGH
1974
Town (15)
Small Part Excluding Core
Residential, Other
Country House

16. WORTLEY
1974
Rural Main Settlement
Bulk of Settlement
Residential, Other
Farmstead

Doncaster

1. ADWICK-LE-STREET,
WOODLANDS
1979
Town (19)
Large Part Excluding Core
Residential, Open Space
Industrial Community, Woodland

2. BARNBURGH
1978
Rural Main Settlement
Including Bulk of Core
Residential
Country House, Farmsteads

3. BAWTRY
1970
Rural Main Settlement,
Pre-industrial Town
Including Bulk of Core
Residential, Other
Country House

4. BRAITHWELL
1979
Rural Main Settlement
Including Bulk of Core
Residential
Farmsteads, Farmland

5. BURGHWALLIS
1978
Rural Main Settlement
Including Bulk of Core
Residential
Country House, Farmstead

6. CAMPSALL
1971
Rural Other Settlement
Including Bulk of Core
Residential
Country House, Park

7. CLIFTON
1977
Rural Other Settlement
Bulk of Settlement
Residential
Farmstead

8. CONISBROUGH
1973
Town (16)
Including Bulk of Core
Residential, Other
Castle, Stream

SOUTH YORKSHIRE

9. DONCASTER, BENNETTHORPE
   1977
   Town (82), Pre-industrial Town
   Including Part of Core
   Open Space, Shops/Offices
   Town House

10. DONCASTER, CHRIST CHURCH
    1977
    Town (82), Pre-industrial Town
    Including Part of Core
    Residential, Other

11. DONCASTER, HIGH STREET
    1978 (1974) Amended
    Town (82), Pre-industrial Town
    Including Part of Core
    Shops/Offices

12. DONCASTER, MARKET PLACE
    1974
    Town (82), Pre-industrial Town
    Including Part of Core
    Shops/Offices

13. DONCASTER, SOUTH PARADE
    1979
    Town (82), Pre-industrial Town
    Including Part of Core
    Shops/Offices, Other

14. HATFIELD
    1970
    Rural Main Settlement
    Including Bulk of Core
    Residential
    Country House

15. HICKLETON
    1971
    Rural Main Settlement
    Bulk of Settlement
    Residential
    Country House, Park, Farmstead,
    Woodland

16. HIGH MELTON
    1983
    Rural Main Settlement
    Bulk of Settlement
    Residential
    Country House(College), Park

17. HOOTON PAGNELL
    1970
    Rural Main Settlement
    Bulk of Settlement
    Residential
    Country House, Park, Farmsteads,
    Tithe Barn

18. LOVERSALL
    1979
    Rural Main Settlement
    Bulk of Settlement
    Residential
    Country House, Park, Streams

19. OWSTON
    1978
    Rural Main Settlement
    Bulk of Settlement
    Residential
    Country House, Park, Farmland

20. SPROTBROUGH
    1971
    Rural Main Settlement
    Including Part of Core
    Residential, Open Space

21. SUTTON
    1975
    Rural Other Settlement
    Bulk of Settlement
    Residential
    Farmsteads

22. THORNE
    1968
    Rural Main Settlement
    Including Bulk of Core
    Residential, Open Space, Other
    Castle Mound, Canal

23. TICKHILL
    1970
    Town (5), Pre-industrial Town
    Bulk of Settlement
    Residential, Shops/Offices, Other
    Castle, Mill, Stream

24. WARMSWORTH
    1971
    Rural Main Settlement
    Including Bulk of Core
    Residential, Other

Rotherham

1. ASTON
   1976
   Rural Main Settlement
   Including Bulk of Core
   Residential, Other

2. DALTON PARVA
   1976
   Rural Other Settlement
   Bulk of Settlement
   Residential

3. DINNINGTON
   1976
   Rural Main Settlement
   Including Part of Core
   Residential, Other
   Country House

4. GILDINGWELLS
   1976
   Rural Main Settlement
   Bulk of Settlement
   Residential
   Farmland, Farmsteads

5. GREASBROUGH
   (NR. ROTHERHAM)
   1977
   Urban Village (82)
   Including Bulk of Core
   Residential

6. HARTHILL
   1976
   Rural Main Settlement
   Including Bulk of Core
   Residential, Other
   Farmsteads

7. LAUGHTON-EN-LE-MORTHEN
   1969
   Rural Other Settlement
   Including Part of Core
   Residential
   Castle

8. NORTH ANSTON
   1976
   Rural Main Settlement
   Including Bulk of Core
   Residential
   Country House

9. RAVENFIELD
   1976
   Rural Main Settlement
   Bulk of Settlement
   Residential
   Farmland, Park, Farmsteads

10. ROTHERHAM,
    ALL SAINTS SQUARE
    1969
    Town (82), Pre-industrial Town
    Including Part of Core
    Shops/Offices, Other

11. ROTHERHAM, CLIFTON
    MOUNT / WELLGATE TERRACE
    1969
    Town (82), Pre-industrial Town
    Small Part Excluding Core
    Residential

SOUTH YORKSHIRE

12. ROTHERHAM, MOORGATE
    1977
    Town (82), Pre-industrial Town
    Small Part Excluding Core
    Residential, Other

13. ROTHERHAM, THE CROFTS
    1969
    Town (82), Pre-industrial Town
    Including Part of Core
    Residential

14. SCHOLES (NR. ROTHERHAM)
    1976
    Urban Village (82)
    Bulk of Settlement
    Residential, Open Space
    Farmland, Woodland, Stream,
    Earthwork

15. SOUTH ANSTON
    1976
    Rural Main Settlement
    Including Bulk of Core
    Residential

16. SWINTON
    1977
    Town (15)
    Including Bulk of Core
    Residential, Shops/Offices

17. THORPE HESLEY
    (NR. ROTHERHAM)
    1977 (1976) Amended
    Urban Village (82)
    Including Bulk of Core
    Residential

18. THORPE SALVIN
    1977
    Rural Main Settlement
    Bulk of Settlement
    Residential, Open Space
    Country House, Moated Site

19. TREETON
    1976
    Rural Main Settlement
    Including Bulk of Core
    Residential
    Farmstead

20. WALES
    1976
    Rural Main Settlement
    Including Bulk of Core
    Residential
    Farmsteads

21. WATH-UPON-DEARNE
    1977
    Town (14)
    Including Bulk of Core
    Residential, Shops/Offices
    Canal

22. WENTWORTH
    1979 (1971) Amended
    Rural Main Settlement
    Bulk of Settlement
    Residential
    Almshouses, Farmsteads

23. WHISTON
    1976
    Rural Main Settlement
    Including Bulk of Core
    Residential
    Stream, Farmstead

24. WICKERSLEY
    1976
    Rural Main Settlement
    Including Bulk of Core
    Residential, Other

25. WOODSETTS
    1977
    Rural Main Settlement
    Including Bulk of Core
    Residential
    Country House, Farmsteads

Sheffield

1. BOLSTERSTONE
   (NR. STOCKSBRIDGE)
   1977
   Urban Village (14)
   Bulk of Settlement
   Residential
   Castle, Farmstead

2. BRIGHTHOLMLEE
   1977
   Rural Other Settlement
   Bulk of Settlement
   Residential
   Farmland, Farmstead

3. DORE (NR. SHEFFIELD)
   1971
   Urban Village (477)
   Including Part of Core
   Residential, Open Space

4. ECCLESFIELD
   1977
   Rural Main Settlement
   Including Bulk of Core
   Residential
   Moated Site

5. GRENOSIDE
   1976
   Rural Other Settlement
   Including Bulk of Core
   Residential, Open Space

6. HIGH AND LOW BRADFIELD
   1981
   Rural Main Settlement
   Bulk of Settlement
   Residential, Open Space
   National Park(G)
   River

7. MIDHOPESTONES
   1976
   Rural Other Settlement
   Bulk of Settlement
   Residential
   Farmland, Farmstead

8. SHEFFIELD,
   BEAUCHIEF ABBEY
   1969
   Urban Non Settlement (477)
   Not Applicable
   Open Space
   Abbey

9. SHEFFIELD, BEAUCHIEF HALL
   1969
   Urban Non Settlement (477)
   Not Applicable
   Open Space
   Country House, Park

10. SHEFFIELD, BROOMHALL
    1970
    Town (477), Pre-industrial Town
    Large Part Excluding Core
    Residential

11. SHEFFIELD, BROOMHILL
    1977
    Town (477), Pre-industrial Town
    Large Part Excluding Core
    Residential, Other

12. SHEFFIELD, CATHEDRAL
    1970
    Town (477), Pre-industrial Town
    Including Part of Core
    Shops/Offices, Other
    Cathedral

13. SHEFFIELD, ENDCLIFFE
    1976
    Town (477), Pre-industrial Town
    Small Part Excluding Core
    Residential, Open Space, Other

SOUTH YORKSHIRE

14. SHEFFIELD, FULWOOD
1976
Town (477), Pre-industrial Town
Small Part Excluding Core
Residential, Open Space
River, Woodland

15. SHEFFIELD,
GENERAL CEMETARY
1986
Urban Non-Settlement (477),
Pre-industrial Town
Not Applicable
Cemetary

16. SHEFFIELD, GREENHILL
1971
Town (477), Pre-industrial Town
Small Part Excluding Core
Residential

17. SHEFFIELD, HACKENTHORPE
1976
Town (477), Pre-industrial Town
Small Part Excluding Core
Industrial, Other

18. SHEFFIELD, HANOVER
1978
Town (477), Pre-industrial Town
Small Part Excluding Core
Residential

19. SHEFFIELD, KELHAM ISLAND
1985
Town (477), Pre-industrial Town
Small Part Excluding Core
Industrial
Industrial Monument (Steel Works),
River

20. SHEFFIELD, NORFOLK ROAD
1982
Town (477), Pre-industrial Town
Small Part Excluding Core
Residential
Almshouses

21. SHEFFIELD,
NORTHUMBERLAND ROAD
1982
Town (477), Pre-industrial Town
Small Part Excluding Core
Residential, Other

22. SHEFFIELD, NORTON
1969
Urban Non Settlement (477)
Not Applicable
Residential
Country House, Park, Almshouses,
Ponds

23. SHEFFIELD, RANMOOR
1986 (1973) Amended
Town (477), Pre-industrial Town
Large Part Excluding Core
Residential, Other

24. SHEFFIELD, TOWN HALL
1977
Town (477), Pre-industrial Town
Including Bulk of Core
Shops/Offices

25. SHEFFIELD, WADSLEY
1976
Town (477), Pre-industrial Town
Small Part Excluding Core
Residential

26. TOTLEY (NR. SHEFFIELD)
1973
Urban Village (477)
Bulk of Settlement
Residential, Other
Country House(College)

27. UPPERMIDHOPE
1977
Rural Other Settlement
Bulk of Settlement
Residential
National Park(G)
Farmsteads

28. WHIRLOW (NR. SHEFFIELD)
1977
Urban Non Settlement (477)
Not Applicable
Residential
Country House

DESIGNATION ACTIVITY 1987

Rotherham
- 26 BRAMPTON-EN-LE-MORPHEN
- 7 LAUGHTON-EN-LE-MORPHEN (EXTENSION)

Sheffield
- 11 BROOMHILL (EXTENSION)
- 19 KELHAM ISLAND (EXTENSION)

DESIGNATION ACTIVITY 1988

Sheffield
- 29 NORTON, OAKES PARK

SOUTH YORKSHIRE

FOOTNOTES

Barnsley

12. LANGSETT — Part of the designated area lies in the National Park and this part was designated by the Peak Park Joint Planning Board.

Doncaster

3. BAWTRY — Part of the area designated in 1970 lay within Worksop, Nottinghamshire; but with the change in the alignment of the Rural District county boundary in 1974, the whole of the orginal area was transferred to South Yorkshire.

Rotherham

22. WENTWORTH — The 1979 designation added the secondary settlement of Barrow to the main designated area of Wentworth which remained unaltered.

Sheffield

6. HIGH AND LOW BRADFIELD — The Conservation Area comprises two portions.

TYNE AND WEAR

Gateshead

1. BIRTLEY
   1976
   Rural Main Settlement
   Including Bulk of Core
   Residential, Open Space

2. BLAYDON, BLAYDON BANK
   1975
   Town (31)
   Including Bulk of Core
   Residential, Open Space, Other
   Quarries

3. GATESHEAD, REGENT
   TERRACE / WALKER TERRACE
   1977
   Town (75), Pre-industrial Town
   Including Part of Core
   Shops/Offices, Other

4. LINTZFORD (NR. BLAYDON)
   1976
   Urban Non Settlement (31)
   Not Applicable
   Open Space
   River, Mill, Farmstead, Woodland,
   Meadows

5. RYTON
   1972
   Town (15)
   Including Bulk of Core
   Residential, Open Space, Shops/
   Offices, Other
   Woodland, Lake

6. WHICKHAM
   1974
   Town (32)
   Including Bulk of Core
   Residential, Open Space, Shops/
   Offices, Other
   Town House(Hospital)

Newcastle upon Tyne

1. BRANDLING VILLAGE
   1975
   Town (192), Pre-industrial Town
   Large Part Excluding Core
   Residential, Open Space, Other

2. FRAMLINGTON PLACE
   1975
   Town (192), Pre-industrial Town
   Small Part Excluding Core
   Residential

3. LEAZES
   1974
   Town (192), Pre-industrial Town
   Including Part of Core
   Residential, Open Space, Shops/
   Offices

4. SUMMERHILL
   1975 (1971) Amended
   Town (192), Pre-industrial Town
   Small Part Excluding Core
   Residential, Open Space

5. TOWN CENTRE
   1982 (1968) Amalgamated
   Town (192), Pre-industrial Town
   Including Bulk of Core
   Shops/Offices, Industrial
   River, Wharf, Castle,
   Market Building, Industrial
   Monument(Railway Station/
   Bridge), Bridges

North Tyneside

1. BACKWORTH
   1974
   Urban Village (12)
   Including Bulk of Core
   Residential, Open Space
   Farmsteads

2. EARSDON
   1974
   Urban Village (12)
   Bulk of Settlement
   Residential
   Cemetary, Farmland

3. KILLINGWORTH VILLAGE
   (NR. LONGBENTON)
   1974
   Urban Village (51)
   Bulk of Settlement
   Residential

4. LONGBENTON
   1985
   Town (51)
   Large Part Excluding Core
   Residential, Other

5. NORTH SHIELDS,
   CAMP TERRACE
   1974
   Town (60), Pre-industrial Town
   Small Part Excluding Core
   Residential

6. NORTH SHIELDS, NEW QUAY
   1984
   Town (60), Pre-industrial Town
   Small Part Excluding Core
   Industrial
   Quay, River Estuary

7. NORTH SHIELDS,
   NORTHUMBERLAND SQUARE
   1983 (1974) Amended
   Town (60), Pre-industrial Town
   Including Part of Core
   Residential, Shops/Offices

8. NORTH SHIELDS,
   PRESTON PARK
   1981
   Town (60), Pre-industrial Town
   Small Part Excluding Core
   Residential, Open Space

9. ST. MARYS ISLAND
   (NR. WHITLEY BAY)
   1974
   Urban Non Settlement (35)
   Not Applicable
   Farmland, Marsh, Seafront,
   Lighthouse, Cliffs

10. TYNEMOUTH
    1977 (1971) Amended
    Town (60), Pre-industrial Town
    Including Bulk of Core
    Residential, Open Space, Shops/
    Offices
    Castle, Pier, Seafront, River Estuary,
    Cliffs, Priory

11. WALLSEND,
    WALLSEND GREEN
    1974
    Town (45)
    Including Part of Core
    Residential, Open Space, Shops/
    Offices, Other
    Town House, Park, Green

South Tyneside

1. BOLDON,
   EAST BOLDON NUCLEUS
   1975
   Town (24)
   Including Bulk of Core
   Residential

2. BOLDON,
   WEST BOLDON NUCLEUS
   1975
   Town (24)
   Including Bulk of Core
   Residential, Other

TYNE AND WEAR

3. CLEADON (NR. BOLDON)
   1975
   Urban Village (24)
   Including Bulk of Core
   Residential

4. JARROW, MONKTON
   1975
   Town (27)
   Small Part Excluding Core
   Residential

5. JARROW, ST. PAULS
   1975
   Urban Non Settlement (27)
   Not Applicable
   Open Space
   Abbey, River

6. SOUTH SHIELDS,
   MARINERS COTTAGES
   1981
   Town (87), Pre-industrial Town
   Small Part Excluding Core
   Residential
   Almshouses

7. SOUTH SHIELDS, MILL DAM
   1981
   Town (87), Pre-industrial Town
   Small Part Excluding Core
   Residential, Industrial, Other
   River, Quay

8. SOUTH SHIELDS, WESTOE
   1975 (1971) Amended
   Town (87), Pre-industrial Town
   Including Part of Core
   Residential, Shops/Offices

9. WHITBURN (NR. BOLDON)
   1971
   Urban Village (24)
   Including Bulk of Core
   Residential, Open Space, Other
   Country Houses, Avenue, Farmland

Sunderland

1. HOUGHTON-LE-SPRING, EAST
   1976
   Town (31)
   Including Part of Core
   Residential, Shops/Offices

2. HOUGHTON-LE-SPRING, WEST
   1976
   Town (31)
   Including Part of Core
   Residential, Shops/Offices

3. NEWBOTTLE
   (NR. HOUGHTON-LE-SPRING)
   1976
   Urban Village (31)
   Including Bulk of Core
   Residential

4. OLD SUNDERLAND, EAST END
   1969
   Town (196), Pre-industrial Town
   Small Part Excluding Core
   Residential, Open Space, Other

5. RYHOPE VILLAGE
   (NR. SUNDERLAND)
   1969
   Urban Village (196)
   Including Part of Core
   Residential
   Green, Farmsteads

6. SILKSWORTH
   (NR. SUNDERLAND)
   1969
   Urban Non Settlement (196)
   Not Applicable
   Residential
   Country House, Park, Pond

7. SUNDERLAND, ASHBROOKE
   1969
   Town (196), Pre-industrial Town
   Including Bulk of Core
   Residential, Open Space, Shops/
   Offices, Other

8. SUNDERLAND,
   BISHOPSWEARMOUTH
   1969
   Town (196), Pre-industrial Town
   Including Part of Core
   Shops/Offices, Other

9. SUNDERLAND, CENTRAL
   1969
   Town (196), Pre-industrial Town
   Including Part of Core
   Residential, Shops/Offices

10. THE BENTS COTTAGES
    (NR. SUNDERLAND)
    1969
    Urban Non Settlement (196)
    Not Applicable
    Residential
    Seafront, Country House

11. WASHINGTON,
    WASHINGTON VILLAGE
    1976
    Town (46)
    Including Bulk of Core
    Residential, Other

DESIGNATION ACTIVITY 1987

Newcastle upon Tyne	6	SOUTH JESMOND
	7	NORTHUMBERLAND GARDENS
	5	TOWN CENTRE (EXTENSION)
Sunderland	7	ASHBROOKE (EXTENSION)

DESIGNATION ACTIVITY 1988

Gateshead	7	COATSWORTH
	5	RYTON (EXTENSION)
	6	WHICKHAM (EXTENSION)
South Tyneside	10	SOUTH SHIELDS, CLEADON PUMPING STATION
	8	SOUTH SHIELDS, WESTOE (EXTENSION)

TYNE AND WEAR

FOOTNOTES

Gateshead

4. LINTZFORD
   (NR BLAYDON)   This Conservation Area extends into Derwentside, DURHAM.

Newcastle upon Tyne

5. TOWN CENTRE   Amalgamating BIGG MARKET / GROAT MARKET (1971), CATHEDRAL / CASTLE (1968), DOBSON GRAINGER AREA (1968).

North Tyneside

10. TYNEMOUTH   The town has two nuclei, both designated, Tynemouth and North Shields. Details as to scale of coverage, which rlate to the core, refer to the relevant nucleus.

WEST YORKSHIRE

Bradford

1. ADDINGHAM
   1977
   Rural Main Settlement
   Including Bulk of Core
   Residential, Industrial
   River

2. BAILDON
   1981
   Town (16)
   Including Bulk of Core
   Residential, Shops/Offices,
   Industrial

3. BAILDON, STATION ROAD
   1981
   Town (16)
   Small Part Excluding Core
   Residential

4. BINGLEY
   1973
   Town (28), Pre-industrial Town
   Including Bulk of Core
   Open Space, Shops/Offices,
   Industrial
   River

5. BRADFORD,
   APSLEY CRESCENT
   1975
   Town (281), Pre-industrial Town
   Small Part Excluding Core
   Residential

6. BRADFORD,
   CATHEDRAL PRECINCT
   1982 (1974) Amended
   Town (281), Pre-industrial Town
   Including Part of Core
   Industrial, Other
   Cathedral

7. BRADFORD, CENTRAL AREA
   1982 (1974) Amended
   Town (281), Pre-industrial Town
   Including Part of Core
   Shops/Offices

8. BRADFORD, ELDON PLACE
   1982 (1973) Amended
   Town (281), Pre-industrial Town
   Small Part Excluding Core
   Residential

9. BRADFORD, GREAT HORTON
   1978
   Town (281), Pre-industrial Town
   Small Part Excluding Core
   Residential, Other

10. BRADFORD, HEATON ESTATES
    1981
    Town (281)
    Large Part Excluding Core
    Residential, Other

11. BRADFORD, HODGSON'S FOLD
    1975
    Town (281), Pre-industrial Town
    Small Part Excluding Core
    Residential

12. BRADFORD, IDLE
    1978
    Town (281), Pre-industrial Town
    Small Part Excluding Core
    Residential, Other

13. BRADFORD, LITTLE GERMANY
    1982 (1974) Amended
    Town (281), Pre-industrial Town
    Including Part of Core
    Industrial, Other

14. BRADFORD, LITTLE HORTON
    GREEN
    1973
    Town (281), Pre-industrial Town
    Small Part Excluding Core
    Residential, Other

15. BRADFORD, LITTLE HORTON
    LANE
    1980 (1979) Amended
    Town (281), Pre-industrial Town
    Large Part Excluding Core
    Residential

16. BRADFORD, MANNINGHAM,
    ST. PAULS
    1975
    Town (281), Pre-industrial Town
    Small Part Excluding Core
    Residential

17. BRADFORD,
    NORTH PARK ROAD
    1975
    Town (281), Pre-industrial Town
    Large Part Excluding Core
    Residential, Open Space, Industrial

18. BRADFORD,
    SOUTHFIELD SQUARE
    1980
    Town (281), Pre-industrial Town
    Small Part Excluding Core
    Residential

19. BRADFORD, UNDERCLIFFE
    CEMETARY
    1984
    Urban Non-Settlement (281)
    Not Applicable
    Cemetary

20. BRADFORD, WHETLEY GROVE
    1977
    Town (281), Pre-industrial Town
    Small Part Excluding Core
    Residential

21. BRUNTHWAITE (NR SILSDEN)
    1977
    Urban Village (7)
    Bulk of Settlement
    Residential
    Stream

22. BURLEY IN WHARFEDALE
    (NR ILKLEY)
    1977
    Urban Village (24)
    Including Bulk of Core
    Residential, Open Space
    Country House, Park, Mill, River

23. CLAYTON (NR. BRADFORD)
    1977
    Urban Village (281)
    Including Bulk of Core
    Residential, Other

24. CULLINGWORTH
    (NR. BINGLEY)
    1975
    Urban Village (28)
    Including Part of Core
    Residential, Other

25. EAST MORTON
    (NR. KEIGHLEY)
    1977 (1970) Amended
    Urban Village (57)
    Including Bulk of Core
    Residential
    Mill, Pond

26. ESHOLT (NR. BRADFORD)
    1973
    Urban Village (281)
    Bulk of Settlement
    Residential
    Woodland, Moated Site, Farmstead

WEST YORKSHIRE

7. BRAMHAM
   1975
   Rural Main Settlement
   Including Bulk of Core
   Residential, Open Space, Other
   Stream, Country House, Park, Farmstead

8. CALVERLEY (NR. PUDSEY)
   1984
   Urban Village (33)
   Including Bulk of Core
   Residential, Other

9. CALVERLEY BRIDGE (NR. PUDSEY)
   1984
   Urban Non-Settlement (33)
   Not Applicable
   River, Canal

10. CLIFFORD
    1973
    Rural Main Settlement
    Including Bulk of Core
    Residential, Other
    Stream

11. EAST KESWICK
    1974
    Rural Main Settlement
    Including Bulk of Core
    Residential
    Stream, Meadows

12. FARNLEY UPPER MOORSIDE (NR. LEEDS)
    1975
    Urban Village (449)
    Bulk of Settlement
    Residential
    Farmstead

13. GUISLEY TOWNGATE
    1985
    Twin Town (31)
    Including Bulk of Core
    Residential, Industrial, Other
    Town House, Pond

14. HAREWOOD
    1976
    Rural Main Settlement
    Bulk of Settlement
    Residential, Open Space
    Castle, Farmland, Woodland

15. HORSFORTH
    1975 (1972) Amended
    Town (19)
    Including Bulk of Core
    Residential, Shops/Offices

16. LEEDS, BLENHEIM SQUARE
    1978 (1972) Amended
    Town (449), Pre-industrial Town
    Small Part Excluding Core
    Residential, Other

17. LEEDS, BRAMLEY, HILL TOP
    1974
    Town (449), Pre-industrial Town
    Small Part Excluding Core
    Other

18. LEEDS, BURLEY VILLAGE
    1986
    Town (449), Pre-industrial Town
    Small Part Excluding Core
    Residential, Open Space, Other

19. LEEDS, CANAL WHARF
    1979
    Town (449), Pre-industrial Town
    Including Part of Core
    Industrial
    Canal, River

20. LEEDS, CHAPEL ALLERTON
    1973
    Town (449), Pre-industrial Town
    Small Part Excluding Core
    Residential, Other

21. LEEDS, CHAPEL TOWN STREET
    1974
    Town (449), Pre-industrial Town
    Small Part Excluding Core
    Residential, Other

22. LEEDS, CITY CENTRE
    1981 (1972) Amalgamated
    Town (449), Pre-industrial Town
    Including Bulk of Core
    Residential, Open Space, Shops/Offices, Industrial, Other
    River

23. LEEDS, CLARENDON ROAD
    1974
    Town (449), Pre-industrial Town
    Small Part Excluding Core
    Residential, Other

24. LEEDS, HANOVER SQUARE / WOODHOUSE SQUARE
    1973
    Town (449), Pre-industrial Town
    Small Part Excluding Core
    Residential, Other

25. LEEDS, HEADINGLEY
    1984 (1972) Amalgamated
    Town (449), Pre-industrial Town
    Large Part Excluding Core
    Residential, Other
    Town Houses

26. LEEDS, KIRKSTALL ABBEY
    1974
    Town (449), Pre-industrial Town
    Small Part Excluding Core
    Residential, Open Space
    Abbey, Park, River

27. LEEDS, MEANWOOD
    1986
    Town (449), Pre-industrial Town
    Large Part Excluding Core
    Open Space
    River, Woodland

28. LEEDS, MEANWOOD, TANNERY SQUARE
    1972
    Town (449), Pre-industrial Town
    Small Part Excluding Core
    Residential

29. LEEDS, QUEEN SQUARE
    1973
    Town (449), Pre-industrial Town
    Including Part of Core
    Shops/Offices, Other

30. LEEDS, ROUNDHAY PARK
    1985 (1974) Amended
    Town (449), Pre-industrial Town
    Large Part Excluding Core
    Residential, Open Space, Other
    Golf Course, Lake, Wooded Gorge, Farmsteads

31. LEEDS, SEACROFT - DAWSONS COURT
    1972
    Town (449), Pre-industrial Town
    Small Part Excluding Core
    Residential

32. LEEDS, WHITKIRK
    1973
    Town (449), Pre-industrial Town
    Small Part Excluding Core
    Other

33. LEEDS, WOODHOUSE LANE
    1979
    Town (449), Pre-industrial Town
    Small Part Excluding Core
    Residential, Other
    Cemetary

WEST YORKSHIRE

34. LITTLE LONDON
   (NR. YEADON)
   1977 (1973) Amended
   Urban Village (31)
   Bulk of Settlement
   Residential

35. METHLEY (NR. ROTHWELL)
   1975
   Urban Village (29)
   Including Bulk of Core
   Residential, Open Space, Other

36. MORLEY,
   COMMERCIAL STREET
   1975
   Town (44)
   Including Bulk of Core
   Residential, Open Space, Shops/
   Offices, Industrial

37. MORLEY, DARTMOUTH PARK
   1975
   Town (44)
   Large Part Excluding Core
   Residential, Open Space

38. OTLEY
   1978 (1970) Amended
   Town (14), Pre-industrial Town
   Including Bulk of Core
   Residential, Shops/Offices
   River, Bridge

39. OULTON (NR. ROTHWELL)
   1975
   Urban Village (29)
   Including Bulk of Core
   Residential, Other

40. PARKGATE (NR. GUISLEY)
   1985
   Urban Non-Settlement (31)
   Not Applicable
   Residential
   Park, Farmstead

41. PUDSEY
   1985
   Town (33)
   Including Bulk of Core
   Residential, Open Space, Shops/
   Offices

42. PUDSEY, FULNECK
   1972
   Town (33)
   Small Part Excluding Core
   Residential, Open Space, Other
   Planned Community

43. RODLEY (NR. PUDSEY)
   1975
   Urban Village (33)
   Including Part of Core
   Residential
   Canal, Farmstead, Stream

44. ROTHWELL
   1976
   Town (29), Pre-industrial Town
   Including Part of Core
   Residential, Open Space, Other
   Farmstead, Stream

45. SCARCROFT
   1975
   Rural Main Settlement
   Including Part of Core
   Residential, Open Space
   Country House, Park, Farmstead

46. SHADWELL (NR. LEEDS)
   1973
   Urban Village (449)
   Including Bulk of Core
   Residential, Other
   Farmstead

47. THORNER
   1970
   Rural Main Settlement
   Including Bulk of Core
   Residential
   Farmstead

48. WETHERBY
   1971
   Rural Main Settlement,
   Pre-industrial Town
   Including Part of Core
   Residential, Other
   River, Meadows, Bridge

49. WOODHALL HILLS
   (NR. PUDSEY)
   1984
   Urban Non-Settlement (33)
   Not Applicable
   Farmsteads. Woodlands

50. YEADON
   1973
   Twin Town (31)
   Including Bulk of Core
   Residential, Shops/Offices

Wakefield

1. BADSWORTH
   1972
   Rural Main Settlement
   Bulk of Settlement
   Residential
   Farmsteads

2. CRIGGLESTONE,
   CHAPELTHORPE
   1969
   Rural Other Settlement
   Including Bulk of Core
   Residential
   Country House, Park

3. HEATH
   1972
   Rural Main Settlement
   Bulk of Settlement
   Residential, Open Space
   Country House, Park, Common,
   Heath, Farmstead

4. HIGH ACKWORTH
   1975
   Rural Main Settlement
   Bulk of Settlement
   Residential, Other
   Farmland, School, Farmstead

5. HORBURY
   1973
   Town (9)
   Including Bulk of Core
   Residential, Shops/Offices

6. KIRKTHORPE
   1981
   Rural Other Settlement
   Including Bulk of Core
   Residential
   Almshouses

7. KNOTTINGLEY
   1975
   Town (16)
   Including Bulk of Core
   Residential, Other
   Canal, River

8. NEWMILLERDAM
   1970
   Rural Other Settlement
   Bulk of Settlement
   Residential
   Stream

9. NORMANTON
   1975
   Town (17)
   Including Part of Core
   Residential, Other

10. OSSETT
    1980
    Town (20)
    Including Bulk of Core
    Residential, Shops/Offices

WEST YORKSHIRE

11. PONTEFRACT, CASTLE
1977 (1969) Amended
Town (33), Pre-industrial Town
Including Part of Core
Shops/Offices
Castle

12. PONTEFRACT, MARKET PLACE
1977 (1969) Amended
Town (33), Pre-industrial Town
Including Bulk of Core
Shops/Offices

13. WAKEFIELD, CITY CENTRE
1980 (1968) Amalgamated
Town (61), Pre-industrial Town
Including Part of Core
Residential, Shops/Offices, Other

14. WAKEFIELD, LOWER WESTGATE
1975
Town (61), Pre-industrial Town
Including Part of Core
Shops/Offices

15. WAKEFIELD, SANDAL CASTLE
1972
Urban Non Settlement (61)
Not Applicable
Castle

16. WAKEFIELD, SOUTH PARADE
1968
Town (61), Pre-industrial Town
Including Part of Core
Residential, Shops/Offices

17. WENTBRIDGE
1981
Rural Other Settlement
Bulk of Settlement
Residential
River, Meadows, Farmstead

18. WEST BRETTON
1970
Rural Main Settlement
Bulk of Settlement
Residential, Open Space
Farmstead

19. WHITWOOD (NR. CASTLEFORD)
1975
Urban Village (36)
Large Part Excluding Core
Residential

20. WOOLLEY
1970
Rural Main Settlement
Bulk of Settlement
Residential
Avenue, Farmstead

21. WOOLLEY HOME FARM
1976
Rural Non Settlement
Not Applicable
Other
Country House(College), Park

22. WRAGBY
1975
Rural Other Settlement
Bulk of Settlement
Residential
Farmstead

DESIGNATION ACTIVITY 1987

Calderdale   5   HEBDEN BRIDGE   (EXTENSION)

Kirklees   53   BATLEY, STATION ROAD

Leeds
- 51 BRAMLEY, TOWN STREET
- 52 MORLEY, STANK HALL
- 53 BRAMLEY, HOUGH LANE
- 54 MOORLANDS
- 39 OULTON (NR ROTHWELL) (EXTENSION)
- 41 PUDSEY (EXTENSION)
- 44 ROTHWELL (EXTENSION)

DESIGNATION ACTIVITY 1988

Bradford   53   LEEDS AND LIVERPOOL CANAL

Leeds
- 55 YEADON, ROWDON, LOW GREEN
- 56 YEADON, ROWDON, CRAGG WOOD
- 34 LITTLE LONDON (NR YEADON) (EXTENSION)

WEST YORKSHIRE

FOOTNOTES

Bradford

7. BRADFORD, CENTRAL AREA — Formerly designated as WOOL EXCHANGE.

13. BRADFORD, LITTLE GERMANY — Formerly designated as VICAR LANE.

Kirklees

27. HUDDERSFIELD, ST. GEORGES SQUARE — The designated area remains a distinct Conservation Area within the larger area designated later as HUDDERSFIELD TOWN CENTRE.

Leeds

22. LEEDS, CITY CENTRE — Amalgamating CENTRAL PRECINCT (1973) [Itself an amalgamation of ALBION STREET / HEADROW / BRIGGATE (1973) and QUEEN VICTORIA STREET /KING EDWARD STREET (1972)], PARK SQUARE (1972), CENTRAL AREA [or DUNCAN STREET] (1973), YORK PLACE / PARK PLACE (1974), PARISH CHURCH PRECINCT (1977) and CIVIC AREA / GREAT GEORGE STREET (1978).

25. LEEDS, HEADINGLEY — Amalgamating FAR HEADINGLEY (1972) [originally designated as COTTAGE ROAD], HEADINGLEY HILL (1973), CARDIGAN ROAD (1973), CHAPEL STREET (1974) and WOOD LANE / GROVE LANE (1975).

Wakefield

13. WAKEFIELD, CITY CENTRE — Amalgamating ST JOHNS (1968), WENTWORTH TERRACE (1975), UPPER WESTGATE (1975), CATHEDRAL (1975) and WOOD STREET (1975).

17. WENTBRIDGE — This Conservation Area extends into Selby, NORTH YORKSHIRE.

CHESHIRE

Chester

1. ALDERSLEY GREEN
   1973
   Rural Other Settlement
   Bulk of Settlement
   Residential
   Farmstead, Stream, Pond

2. ALDFORD
   1974
   Rural Main Settlement
   Bulk of Settlement
   Residential
   Castle Mound, River,
   Industrial Monument (Bridge)

3. ASHTON
   1979
   Rural Main Settlement
   Bulk of Settlement
   Residential
   Farmstead

4. BARTON
   1973
   Rural Main Settlement
   Bulk of Settlement
   Residential
   Farmstead

5. BEESTON
   1980
   Rural Main Settlement
   Bulk of Settlement
   Residential
   Castle, Farmsteads, Farmland,
   Woodland

6. BRUERA
   1979
   Rural Non Settlement
   Not Applicable
   Moated Site

7. BURTON
   1973
   Rural Main Settlement
   Bulk of Settlement
   Residential
   Country House, Farmstead

8. CHESTER CITY
   1985 (1969) Amalgamated
   Town (58), Pre-industrial Town
   Including Bulk of Core
   Residential, Open Space, Shops/
   Offices, Industrial, Other
   River, City Walls, Industrial
   Monument(Station), Bridge,
   Suspension Bridge, Race Course,
   Canal

9. CHESTER, BOUGHTON AND
   THE MEADOWS
   1979
   Town (58), Pre-industrial Town
   Large Part Excluding Core
   Residential, Open Space, Other
   River, Meadows

10. CHESTER, CURZON PARK
    1979
    Town (58), Pre-industrial Town
    Large Part Excluding Core
    Residential, Open Space
    River

11. CHESTER, EGERTON STREET
    1980
    Town (58), Pre-industrial Town
    Small Part Excluding Core
    Residential, Industrial
    Canal

12. CHESTER, FLOOKERSBROOK
    1976
    Town (58), Pre-industrial Town
    Small Part Excluding Core
    Residential, Open Space

13. CHESTER, HANDBRIDGE
    1979
    Town (58), Pre-industrial Town
    Small Part Excluding Core
    Residential
    River, Bridge

14. CHESTER, QUEENS PARK
    1979
    Town (58), Pre-industrial Town
    Small Part Excluding Core
    Residential

15. CHRISTLETON
    1973
    Rural Main Settlement
    Including Bulk of Core
    Residential, Open Space
    Canal, Country House, Pond,
    Meadows

16. CHURTON
    1973
    Rural Main Settlement
    Including Bulk of Core
    Residential
    Country House, Park, Farmsteads,
    Pond

17. CLOTTON
    1980
    Rural Main Settlement
    Bulk of Settlement
    Residential
    Country House, Farmsteads

18. CODDINGTON
    1973
    Rural Main Settlement
    Bulk of Settlement
    Residential
    River, Mill, Farmsteads, Pond,
    Meadows, Earthwork

19. DUNHAM-ON-THE-HILL
    1979
    Rural Main Settlement
    Bulk of Settlement
    Residential
    Farmsteads

20. ECCLESTON
    1979
    Rural Main Settlement
    Bulk of Settlement
    Residential
    River, Woodland, Country House,
    Earthwork, Meadows

21. ELTON
    1979
    Rural Main Settlement
    Including Bulk of Core
    Residential
    Farmsteads

22. FARNDON
    1972
    Rural Main Settlement
    Including Bulk of Core
    Residential, Other
    River, Farmstead, Bridge

23. GREAT BARROW
    1979
    Rural Main Settlement
    Bulk of Settlement
    Residential, Open Space
    Country House, Park, Mill, River,
    Farmstead

CHESHIRE

24. HANDLEY
1973
Rural Main Settlement
Bulk of Settlement
Residential

25. HARTHILL
1973
Rural Main Settlement
Bulk of Settlement
Residential
Farmstead

26. KELSALL
1980
Rural Main Settlement
Including Part of Core
Residential
Farmstead

27. LEDSHAM
1979
Rural Main Settlement
Bulk of Settlement
Residential
Farmstead

28. LITTLE BARROW
1980
Rural Other Settlement
Bulk of Settlement
Residential
Farmsteads

29. MALPAS
1981 (1969) Amended
Rural Main Settlement,
Pre-industrial Town
Including Bulk of Core
Residential, Other
Castle, Camp

30. PUDDINGTON
1981 (1980) Amended
Rural Main Settlement
Bulk of Settlement
Residential
Country Houses, Parks, Moated Site

31. SAIGHTON
1979
Rural Main Settlement
Bulk of Settlement
Residential
Country House

32. SAUGHALL
1982
Rural Main Settlement
Including Part of Core
Residential

33. SHEAF FARM
1980
Rural Non Settlement
Not Applicable
Farmstead

34. SHOTWICK
1974
Rural Main Settlement
Bulk of Settlement
Residential
Country House

35. STOAK
1979
Rural Main Settlement
Bulk of Settlement
Residential
Farmstead

36. TARVIN
1973
Rural Main Settlement
Including Bulk of Core
Residential, Other
River, Meadows

37. TATTENHALL
1986 (1970) Amended
Rural Main Settlement
Including Bulk of Core
Residential, Open Space, Industrial, Other
Country Houses, Mill, Stream

38. TILSTON
1973
Rural Main Settlement
Including Bulk of Core
Residential

39. TIVERTON
1973
Rural Main Settlement
Bulk of Settlement
Residential

40. WAVERTON
1979
Rural Main Settlement
Bulk of Settlement
Residential
Farmstead

Congleton

1. ALSAGER
1981
Town (11)
Small Part Excluding Core
Residential

2. CONGLETON, HIGH STREET
1980
Town (24), Pre-industrial Town
Including Part of Core
Shops/Offices

3. CONGLETON, MOODY SREET
1969
Town (24), Pre-industrial Town
Including Part of Core
Residential, Shops/Offices

4. CONGLETON, SWAN BANK
1969
Town (24), Pre-industrial Town
Including Part of Core
Residential, Shops/Offices

5. HOLMES CHAPEL
1974
Rural Main Settlement
Including Part of Core
Residential, Other

6. MIDDLEWICH
1981
Town (8), Pre-industrial Town
Including Bulk of Core
Shops/Offices

7. NEWBOLD ASTBURY
1970
Rural Main Settlement
Bulk of Settlement
Residential
Green, Moated Site

8. SANDBACH, HIGHTOWN
1976
Town (15)
Including Part of Core
Shops/Offices

9. SANDBACH, MARKET PLACE
1970
Town (15)
Including Part of Core
Residential, Shops/Offices
River

Crewe and Nantwich

1. ACTON
1984
Rural Main Settlement
Bulk of Settlement
Residential
Moated Site, Farmland

CHESHIRE

2. ASTON
1973
Rural Main Settlement
Bulk of Settlement
Residential

3. AUDLEM
1981 (1969) Amended
Rural Main Settlement
Including Part of Core
Residential, Other
Canal

4. AUDLEM WOORE ROAD
1981
Rural Main Settlement
Including Part of Core
Residential

5. BARTHOMLEY
1969
Rural Main Settlement
Bulk of Settlement
Residential
Farmstead, Stream, Meadows

6. CHURCH MINSHULL
1969
Rural Main Settlement
Bulk of Settlement
Residential
River, Mill, Farmstead

7. CREWE GREEN
1984
Rural Main Settlement
Bulk of Settlement
Residential, Open Space
Green

8. ENGLESEA BROOK
1984
Rural Other Settlement
Bulk of Settlement
Residential
Farmstead

9. HIGHER BUNBURY
1973
Rural Main Settlement
Including Bulk of Core
Residential

10. LOWER BUNBURY
1973
Rural Other Settlement
Bulk of Settlement
Residential

11. MARBURY
1973
Rural Main Settlement
Bulk of Settlement
Residential

12. NANTWICH
1973 (1969) Amended
Town (12), Pre-industrial Town
Including Bulk of Core
Residential, Shops/Offices
River, Mill

13. PECKFORTON
1973
Rural Main Settlement
Bulk of Settlement
Residential
Farmstead

14. WARMINGHAM
1984
Rural Main Settlement
Bulk of Settlement
Other
River, Bridge, Earthwork, Farmstead

15. WESTON
1984
Rural Main Settlement
Bulk of Core
Residential

16. WRENBURY
1973
Rural Main Settlement
Including Bulk of Core
Residential, Open Space
Canal, Mill, Green, River, Bridge

17. WYBUNBURY
1981
Rural Main Settlement
Including Bulk of Core
Residential
Moated Sites, Woodland, Meadows, River

Ellesmere Port and Neston

1. BURTON (NR. NESTON)
1974
Urban Village (18)
Including Bulk of Core
Residential, Other
Country House(College), Park

2. ELLESMERE PORT DOCKS
1979 (1975) Amended
Urban Non Settlement (63)
Not Applicable
Industrial Monument (Docks),
Canal, River Estuary

3. INCE (NR. ELLESMERE PORT)
1969
Urban Village (63)
Including Bulk of Core
Residential
Park, Meadow, Farmstead

4. NESS (NR. NESTON)
1984
Urban Village (18)
Including Bulk of Core
Residential

5. NESTON
1980
Town (18)
Including Bulk of Core
Residential, Shops/Offices

6. NESTON, PARKGATE
1973
Town (18)
Including Bulk of Core
Residential, Other
River Estuary

7. WILLASTON (NR. NESTON)
1969
Urban Village (18)
Including Bulk of Core
Residential, Other

Halton

1. DARESBURY
1969
Rural Main Settlement
Bulk of Settlement
Residential

2. HALE
1969
Rural Main Settlement
Including Part of Core
Residential

3. HALE, HALE ROAD
1982
Rural Main Settlement
Large Part Excluding Core
Residential
Woodland

4. HALTON VILLAGE
(NR. RUNCORN)
1970
Urban Village (64)
Including Bulk of Core
Residential, Open Space
Castle

CHESHIRE

5. MOORE
1976
Rural Main Settlement
Bulk of Settlement
Residential

6. RUNCORN, HIGHER RUNCORN
1975
Town (64)
Large Part Excluding Core
Residential

7. WIDNES, WESTBANK
1978
Town (54)
Small Part Excluding Core
Open Space, Other
River

Macclesfield

1. ALDERLEY EDGE
1974
Town (4)
Large Part Excluding Core
Residential

2. ALDERLEY EDGE, ELM GROVE
1986
Town (4)
Small Part Excluding Core
Residential

3. BOLLINGTON
1976
Town (7)
Including Bulk of Core
Residential, Shops/Offices,
Industrial
Industrial Mills, Ponds, River

4. BUTLEY TOWN
1972
Rural Other Settlement
Including Bulk of Core
Residential

5. DISLEY
1973
Rural Main Settlement
Including Part of Core
Open Space, Other

6. GAWSWORTH
1969
Rural Main Settlement
Bulk of Settlement
Residential
Country House, Park, Ponds

7. HIGHER DISLEY
1973
Rural Other Settlement
Including Bulk of Core
Residential
Farmstead

8. KERRIDGE (NR. BOLLINGTON)
1973
Urban Village (7)
Bulk of Settlement
Residential, Other
River, Farmland, Meadows,
  Farmsteads, Country House(Hotel)

9. KNUTSFORD
1977 (1969) Amended
Town (14), Pre-industrial Town
Including Bulk of Core
Residential, Open Space, Shops/
Offices

10. KNUTSFORD, LEGH ROAD
1976
Town (14), Pre-industrial Town
Large Part Excluding Core
Residential

11. MACCLESFIELD CANAL
1975
Urban Non Settlement (47)
Not Applicable
Canal

12. MACCLESFIELD, BARRACKS
SQUARE
1976
Urban Non Settlement (47)
Not Applicable
Residential, Industrial
Military Monument

13. MACCLESFIELD, HIGH STREET
1978
Town (47), Pre-industrial Town
Large Part Excluding Core
Residential, Industrial

14. MACCLESFIELD, HOLLANDS
PLACE / BLACK ROAD
1976
Town (47), Pre-industrial Town
Small Part Excluding Core
Residential
Canal

15. MACCLESFIELD, PARK GREEN
1969
Town (47), Pre-industrial Town
Including Part of Core
Open Space, Industrial

16. MACCLESFIELD, TOWN
CENTRE
1984 (1969) Amended
Town (47), Pre-industrial Town
Including Bulk of Core
Shops/Offices

17. MOBBERLEY
1976
Rural Main Settlement
Including Bulk of Core
Residential, Other
Farmland, Country House(School),
Park, Farmsteads

18. NETHER ALDERLEY
1974
Rural Main Settlement
Including Bulk of Core
Open Space, Other
Country House, Park, Lake,
Woodland, Meadows

19. POTT SHRIGLEY
1980
Rural Main Settlement
Bulk of Settlement
Residential, Open Space
National Park(G)
Woodland, Stream, Country House,
Meadows

20. PRESTBURY
1972
Rural Main Settlement
Including Part of Core
Residential
River, Mill

21. ROSTHERNE
1969
Rural Main Settlement
Bulk of Settlement
Residential, Open Space
Meadow

22. STYAL (NR. WILMSLOW)
1975
Urban Village (30)
Bulk of Settlement
Residential
Country House, Park, River,
Industrial Mill, Wood, Farmland,
Farmsteads

Vale Royal

1. ALVANLEY
1976
Rural Main Settlement
Including Bulk of Core
Residential
Farmsteads

CHESHIRE

2. ARLEY
1979
Rural Other Settlement
Bulk of Settlement
Residential
Country House, Park

3. BARTINGTON
1978
Rural Other Settlement
Bulk of Settlement
Residential

4. BOSTOCK GREEN
1976
Rural Main Settlement
Bulk of Settlement
Residential, Other
Country House(School), Park, Woodland, Lake

5. CUDDINGTON
1977
Rural Main Settlement
Including Bulk of Core
Residential
Country House, Farmstead

6. DAVENHAM
1980 (1974) Amended
Rural Main Settlement
Including Bulk of Core
Residential
Country House, Park

7. EATON
1975
Rural Other Settlement
Bulk of Settlement
Residential
Farmland, Farmsteads

8. FRODSHAM
1977 (1973) Amended
Rural Main Settlement,
Pre-industrial Town
Including Part of Core
Residential, Open Space, Other

9. FRODSHAM, OVERTON
1976
Rural Main Settlement,
Pre-industrial Town
Including Part of Core
Residential, Open Space

10. GREAT BUDWORTH
1981 (1969) Amended
Rural Main Settlement
Bulk of Settlement
Residential, Open Space
Country House, Park, Avenue, Meadow

11. HARTFORD
1974
Rural Main Settlement
Including Bulk of Core
Residential, Open Space

12. HIGHER WHITLEY
1975
Rural Main Settlement
Bulk of Settlement
Residential
Lake

13. KINGSLEY
1976
Rural Main Settlement
Including Bulk of Core
Residential

14. LITTLE BUDWORTH
1975
Rural Main Settlement
Bulk of Settlement
Residential
Lake, Marsh, Meadows

15. LOWER PEOVER
1981
Rural Main Settlement
Including Bulk of Core
Other
River, Meadows

16. LOWER WHITLEY
1977
Rural Other Settlement
Including Bulk of Core
Residential
Farmsteads

17. MARSTON, LION SALTWORKS
1979
Rural Non Settlement
Not Applicable
Industrial
Monument(Salt Works), Canal, Pond, Heath

18. NORTHWICH
1975
Town (17), Pre-industrial Town
Including Bulk of Core
Residential, Open Space, Shops/Offices, Industrial
River, Canal, Locks

19. ONSTON
1978
Rural Other Settlement
Bulk of Settlement
Residential
Farmsteads

20. TARPORLEY
1981 (1972) Amended
Rural Main Settlement,
Pre-industrial Town
Including Bulk of Core
Residential, Other
Woodland, Farmland, Park

21. WEAVERHAM
1981 (1974) Amended
Rural Main Settlement
Including Bulk of Core
Residential, Other

22. WEAVERHAM, WEST ROAD
1981
Rural Main Settlement
Small Part Excluding Core
Residential

23. WHITEGATE (NR. WINSFORD)
1974
Urban Village (27)
Including Bulk of Core
Residential

24. WINSFORD, ST. CHADS
1979
Urban Non Settlement (27)
Not Applicable
Farmstead, Meadows

Warrington

1. GRAPPENHALL
1974
Rural Main Settlement
Including Bulk of Core
Residential, Open Space, Industrial, Other
Canal, Farmstead, Pond, Meadows

2. LYMM, EAGLE BROW
1973
Town (10)
Small Part Excluding Core
Residential

3. LYMM, NEW ROAD
1973
Town (10)
Small Part Excluding Core
Residential

4. LYMM, TOWN CENTRE
1973
Town (10)
Including Bulk of Core
Residential, Open Space, Shops/Offices
Lake, Canal, Town House, Park

CHESHIRE

5. THELWALL
1977
Rural Other Settlement
Including Bulk of Core
Residential, Open Space, Other
School, Canal, Meadows

6. WALTON VILLAGE
1977
Rural Main Settlement
Including Bulk of Core
Residential, Open Space
Park, Canal

7. WARRINGTON, BEWSEY
STREET
1976
Town (57)
Including Part of Core
Residential, Shops/Offices

8. WARRINGTON, BRIDGE
STREET
1980
Town (57)
Including Part of Core
Shops/Offices

9. WARRINGTON, BUTTEMARKET
STREET
1972
Town (57)
Including Part of Core
Shops/Offices

10. WARRINGTON, CHURCH
STREET
1984
Town (57)
Including Part of Core
Shops/Offices

11. WARRINGTON, PALMYRA
SQUARE
1974
Town (57)
Including Part of Core
Open Space, Shops/Offices

12. WARRINGTON, TOWN HALL
1972
Town (57)
Including Part of Core
Open Space, Shops/Offices

DESIGNATION ACTIVITY 1988

Chester
41	HOOLE ROAD	
42	SANDY LANE/DEE BANKS	
10	CURZON PARK	(EXTENSION)

Macclesfield
23	WILMSLOW, ST BARTHOLOMEWS	
24	MACCLESFIELD, CHRISTCHURCH	
25	WILMSLOW, BOLLIN HILL	
26	WILMSLOW, HIGHFIELD	

Vale Royal
10	GREAT BUDWORTH	(EXTENSION)
20	TARPORLEY	(EXTENSION)

FOOTNOTES

Chester

8. CHESTER CITY — Amalgamating CHESTER CITY (1969) and STATION, CHESTER (1980).

Ellesmere Port and Neston

6. NESTON, PARKGATE — The town has two nuclei, both designated (NESTON & PARKGATE). The latter was built as a resort on the sea inlet, formed by the River Dee, but now looks over marsh land. Details as to scale of coverage which relate to the core refer to the relevant nucleus.

Macclesfield

11. MACCLESFIELD CANAL — The Macclesfield Canal is designated throughout its length in Macclesfield District, but not beyond.

19. POTT SHRIGLEY — Holme Wood and the western half of Nab Wood lie outside the National Park.

CHESHIRE

FOOTNOTES continued ....

Vale Royal

2. ARLEY	This Conservation Area extends into Macclesfield, CHESHIRE.
15. LOWER PEOVER	This Conservation Area extends into Macclesfield, CHESHIRE.

CLEVELAND

CLEVELAND

Hartlepool

1. ELWICK
   1975
   Rural Main Settlement
   Bulk of Settlement
   Residential, Open Space
   Country House, Stream, Green, Meadow

2. GREATHAM
   1981 (1974) Amended
   Rural Main Settlement
   Including Bulk of Core
   Residential, Other
   Stream, Farmland, Meadows

3. HARTLEPOOL HEADLAND
   1984 (1969) Amended
   Twin Town (90),
   Pre-industrial Town
   Including Part of Core
   Residential, Open Space, Other
   Seafront, Harbour, Common, Town Wall, Lighthouses, Cliffs

4. SEATON CAREW (NR. WEST HARTLEPOOL)
   1977 (1969) Amended
   Urban Village (90)
   Including Part of Core
   Residential, Open Space
   Seafront, Green

5. WEST HARTLEPOOL, CHURCH STREET
   1984
   Twin Town (90)
   Including Part of Core
   Shops/Offices

6. WEST HARTLEPOOL, THE PARK
   1979
   Twin Town (90)
   Small Part Excluding Core
   Open Space

Langbaurgh

1. BROTTON
   1978
   Twin Town (16)
   Including Bulk of Core
   Residential, Other

2. GUISBOROUGH
   1978 (1971) Amended
   Town (20), Pre-industrial Town
   Including Bulk of Core
   Residential, Shops/Offices
   Priory

3. KIRKLEATHAM (NR. REDCAR)
   1970
   Urban Village (85)
   Bulk of Settlement
   Other
   Country House, Park, Almshouses, Meadows, Woodland

4. LIVERTON (NR. LOFTUS)
   1976
   Urban Village (8)
   Bulk of Settlement
   Residential
   Farmsteads

5. LOFTUS
   1976
   Town (8)
   Including Bulk of Core
   Residential, Open Space, Shops/Offices
   Farmstead

6. MARSKE
   1976
   Twin Town (20)
   Including Bulk of Core
   Residential, Shops/Offices
   Seafront

7. ORMESBY
   (NR. MIDDLESBROUGH)
   1971
   Urban Non Settlement (149)
   Not Applicable
   Open Space
   Country House, Park, Farmstead, Streams

8. SALTBURN-BY-THE-SEA
   1986 (1976) Amended
   Twin Town (20)
   Including Bulk of Core
   Residential, Open Space, Shops/Offices
   Seafront, River, Woodland, Country Houses, Park, Cliffs, Pier, Mill, Stream, Ravine

9. SKELTON
   1979
   Twin Town (16),
   Pre-industrial Town
   Including Bulk of Core
   Residential, Open Space, Other
   Castle, River, Mill, Country House, Park, Pond, Cliffs

10. STAITHES (NR.LOFTUS)
    1972
    See Other (8)
    Not Applicable
    Residential, Open Space
    National Park(E)
    River, Stream, Cliffs

11. UPLEATHAM
    (NR. GUISBOROUGH)
    1976
    Urban Village (20)
    Bulk of Settlement
    Residential
    Meadows

12. WILTON (NR. ESTON)
    1971
    Urban Village (85)
    Bulk of Settlement
    Residential, Open Space
    Country House, Park, Woodland
    Avenue, Park, Golf Course

13. YEARBY (NR. REDCAR)
    1971
    Urban Village (85)
    Bulk of Settlement
    Residential
    Farmstead, Meadows

Middlesbrough

1. ACKLAM HALL
   1971
   Urban Non Settlement (149)
   Not Applicable
   Open Space, Other
   Avenue, Country House(School), Park, Moated Site

2. LINTHORPE
   1975
   Town (149)
   Small Part Excluding Core
   Residential, Open Space

3. NUNTHORPE HALL
   1975
   Rural Main Settlement
   Bulk of Settlement
   Residential
   Country House, Park, Farmland, Pond

4. QUEENS SQUARE
   1970
   Town (149)
   Including Part of Core
   Shops/Offices

CLEVELAND

5. STAINTON AND THORNTON
(NR. MIDDLESBROUGH)
1974
Urban Village (149)
Including Bulk of Core
Residential
Stream, Meadows, Woodland,
Farmstead

6. ZETLAND ROAD
1983
Town (149)
Including Part of Core
Shops/Offices

Stockton on Tees

1. BILLINGHAM, BILLINGHAM
GREEN
1971
Twin Town (149)
Including Part of Core
Residential, Open Space, Other

2. COWPEN BEWLEY
(NR. BILLINGHAM)
1977
Urban Village (149)
Bulk of Settlement
Residential, Open Space
Green

3. EGGLESCLIFFE
1972
Rural Main Settlement
Including Bulk of Core
Residential, Open Space, Other
Country House, River, Meadows,
Bridge

4. STOCKTON-ON-TEES,
HARTBURN
1971
Twin Town (149),
Pre-industrial Town
Small Part Excluding Core
Residential, Open Space
River, Meadows

5. STOCKTON-ON-TEES, NORTON
1969
Twin Town (149),
Pre-industrial Town
Including Bulk of Core
Residential, Open Space, Shops/
Offices
Green

6. STOCKTON-ON-TEES,
TOWN CENTRE
1974
Twin Town (149),
Pre-industrial Town
Including Bulk of Core
Shops/Offices

7. THORNABY GREEN
1971
Twin Town (149)
Large Part Excluding Core
Open Space
River, Meadows, Woodland

8. WOLVISTON
1972
Rural Main Settlement
Bulk of Settlement
Residential, Open Space
Farmland, Green, Meadows

9. YARM
1979 (1969) Amended
Rural Main Settlement,
Pre-industrial Town
Bulk of Settlement
Residential, Other
River, Friary, Bridge

DESIGNATION ACTIVITY 1987

Stockton-on-Tees　　　10　　BUTE STREET

DESIGNATION ACTIVITY 1988

Langbaurgh　　　14　　REDCAR, COATHAM

FOOTNOTES

Langbaurgh

7. ORMESBY
(NR MIDDLESBROUGH)　　　See Middlesbrough, CLEVELAND.

10. STAITHES
(NR LOFTUS)　　　See also Scarborough, NORTH YORKSHIRE.

CLEVELAND

FOOTNOTES continued ...

Stockton on Tees

5. STOCKTON-ON-TEES, NORTON

The town has two nuclei both designated (STOCKTON and NORTON). Details as to the scale of coverage which relate to the core refer to the relevant nucleus.

CUMBRIA

Allerdale

1. ALLONBY
1976
Rural Main Settlement
Including Bulk of Core
Residential
A.O.N.B.(28)
Seafront, Farmland

2. BLENNERHASSET
1981
Rural Main Settlement
Bulk of Settlement
Residential

3. BOWNESS ON SOLWAY
1981
Rural Main Settlement
Bulk of Settlement
Residential
A.O.N.B.(28)
River Estuary, Roman Fort

4. CALDBECK
1983
Rural Main Settlement
Including Bulk of Core
Residential, Open Space
National Park(C)
River, Green, Pond, Farmstead

5. COCKERMOUTH,
DERWENT AREA
1976 (1970) Amended
Urban Non Settlement (7)
Not Applicable
Open Space, Industrial
River, Meadows, Woodland,
Country House, Park

6. COCKERMOUTH,
DERWENT / COCKER
1970
Urban Non Settlement (7)
Not Applicable
River, Mills

7. COCKERMOUTH, HARRIS PARK
/ LAMPLUGH ROAD
1970
Town (7), Pre-industrial Town
Small Part Excluding Core
Residential, Open Space

8. COCKERMOUTH, MAIN STREET
1970
Town (7), Pre-industrial Town
Including Part of Core
Shops/Offices

9. COCKERMOUTH,
MARKET PLACE / CASTLE
1970
Town (7), Pre-industrial Town
Including Part of Core
Residential, Shops/Offices
Castle, River

10. COCKERMOUTH,
OAKHURST WOOD
1976
Urban Non Settlement (7)
Not Applicable
Open Space
River, Meadows, Woodland

11. COCKERMOUTH,
ST. HELENS STREET
1976
Town (7), Pre-industrial Town
Including Part of Core
Residential, Shops/Offices

12. COCKERMOUTH,
WINDMILL LANE
1976
Urban Non Settlement (7)
Not Applicable
Residential
River, Mill

13. GAMELSBY
1981
Rural Other Settlement
Bulk of Settlement
Residential
Farmsteads, Mill

14. GREYSOUTHEN
1983
Rural Main Settlement
Bulk of Settlement
Residential
Country House, Park, Farmsteads

15. HAYTON
1981
Rural Main Settlement
Bulk of Settlement
Residential
Country House, Farmsteads

16. HESKETT NEWMARKET
1983
Rural Other Settlement
Bulk of Settlement
Residential, Open Space
National Park(C)
Green

17. KESWICK
1981
Town (6), Pre-industrial Town
Including Bulk of Core
Residential, Shops/Offices
National Park(C)
River

18. KIRKBAMPTON
1981
Rural Main Settlement
Bulk of Settlement
Residential
Farmsteads

19. MARYPORT
1986 (1976) Amended
Town (12)
Bulk of Settlement
Residential, Open Space, Shops/
Offices, Industrial
Seafront, Docks, Country House,
Park, River, Roman Fort

20. MAWBRAY
1981
Rural Other Settlement
Bulk of Settlement
Residential
A.O.N.B.(28)
Farmstead

21. PAPCASTLE
1983
Rural Main Settlement
Including Bulk of Core
Residential
River, Roman Fort, Farmland

22. PORT CARLISLE
1981
Rural Other Settlement
Bulk of Settlement
Residential
A.O.N.B.(28)
River Estuary

23. SILLOTH
1978
Rural Main Settlement
Including Bulk of Core
Residential, Open Space
Seafront, Green

24. TORPENHOW
1981
Rural Main Settlement
Bulk of Settlement
Residential
Farmstead

CUMBRIA

25. WEST CURTHWAITE
1981
Rural Other Settlement
Bulk of Settlement
Residential
Country House

26. WESTNEWTON
1981
Rural Main Settlement
Bulk of Settlement
Residential
Stream, Farmsteads, Earthworks

27. WIGTON
1977
Rural Main Settlement
Including Bulk of Core
Residential, Open Space, Other

28. WORKINGTON, BROW TOP
1976
Town (28)
Including Part of Core
Residential, Shops/Offices

29. WORKINGTON,
   MARKET PLACE
1979 (1976) Amended
Town (28)
Including Bulk of Core
Residential, Open Space, Shops/
Offices, Other

Barrow in Furness

1. BARROW-IN-FURNESS,
   ST. GEORGES SQUARE
1983
Town (62)
Including Part of Core
Other

2. BIGGAR
   (NR. BARROW-IN-FURNESS)
1974
Urban Village (62)
Bulk of Settlement
Residential
Seafront, Farmstead

3. DALTON-IN-FURNESS,
   MARKET PLACE
1979 (1973) Amended
Town (11), Pre-industrial Town
Including Bulk of Core
Residential, Shops/Offices, Other

4. FURNESS ABBEY
   (NR. BARROW-IN-FURNESS)
1969
Urban Non Settlement (62)
Not Applicable
Abbey, Stream

5. IRELETH
   (NR. DALTON-IN-FURNESS)
1981
Urban Village (11)
Including Bulk of Core
Residential
Stream, Woodland

6. LINDAL, THE GREEN
   (NR. DALTON-IN-FURNESS)
1981
Urban Village (11)
Including Bulk of Core
Residential
Green

7. NORTH SCALE
   (NR. BARROW-IN-FURNESS)
1981
Urban Village (62)
Including Bulk of Core
Residential
Seafront

Carlisle

1. BRAMPTON
1977 (1973) Amended
Rural Main Settlement,
Pre-industrial Town
Including Bulk of Core
Residential, Open Space, Other
Castle

2. BURGH BY SANDS
1978
Rural Main Settlement
Bulk of Settlement
Residential, Open Space
A.O.N.B.(28)
Roman Wall

3. CARLISLE, BOTCHERBY,
   VICTORIA ROAD
1968
Town (72), Pre-industrial Town
Small Part Excluding Core
Residential

4. CARLISLE, BOTCHERBY,
   WOOD STREET
1968
Town (72), Pre-industrial Town
Small Part Excluding Core
Residential

5. CARLISLE, CITY CENTRE
1984 (1968) Amalgamated
Town (72), Pre-industrial Town
Including Part of Core
Shops/Offices
Castle, Law Courts

6. CARLISLE, HOLM HEAD
1968
Urban Non Settlement (72)
Not Applicable
River, Meadows

7. DALSTON
1980
Rural Main Settlement
Including Bulk of Core
Residential, Open Space, Other
Green, River

8. GREAT CORBY
1978
Rural Other Settlement
Bulk of Settlement
Residential, Open Space, Other
River, Woodland, Country House

9. LONGBURGH
1978
Rural Other Settlement
Bulk of Settlement
Residential
A.O.N.B.(28)
Farmstead, Farmland

10. TARRABY
1969
Rural Non Settlement
Not Applicable
Residential
Roman Wall, Farmsteads

11. WETHERAL
1977
Rural Main Settlement
Including Bulk of Core
Residential
Priory, River

Copeland

1. BECKERMET
1979
Rural Other Settlement
Including Bulk of Core
Residential
Stream

CUMBRIA

2. EGREMONT
1985
Rural Main Settlement,
Pre-industrial Town
Including Bulk of Core
Other
Castle

3. RAVENGLASS
1981
Rural Other Settlement,
Pre-industrial Town
Bulk of Settlement
Residential
National Park(C)
River Estuary

4. ST. BEES
1976
Rural Main Settlement
Including Bulk of Core
Residential, Open Space, Other
Priory

5. WHITEHAVEN, CORKICKLE
1969
Town (27), Pre-industrial Town
Small Part Excluding Core
Residential

6. WHITEHAVEN, HENSINGHAM
1969
Town (27), Pre-industrial Town
Small Part Excluding Core
Residential, Other

7. WHITEHAVEN, HIGH STREET /
WELLINGTON ROW
1969
Town (27), Pre-industrial Town
Including Part of Core
Residential, Other

8. WHITEHAVEN, TOWN CENTRE
1974 (1969) Amended
Town (27), Pre-industrial Town
Including Bulk of Core
Residential, Shops/Offices,
Industrial
Harbour

Eden

1. ALSTON
1976
Rural Main Settlement,
Pre-industrial Town
Including Bulk of Core
Residential, Other
A.O.N.B.(23)

2. APPLEBY
1981 (1969) Amended
Town (2), Pre-industrial Town
Including Bulk of Core
Residential, Open Space, Other
River, Meadows, Castle, Mill

3. ASKHAM
1981
Rural Main Settlement
Bulk of Settlement
Residential, Open Space
National Park(C)
Green, River, Country House, Mill

4. CHURCH BROUGH
1969
Rural Main Settlement,
Pre-industrial Town
Bulk of Settlement
Residential, Open Space, Other
Roman Fort/Castle, River, Common

5. HARTSOP (NR.AMBLESIDE)
1985
Urban Village (7)
Bulk of Settlement
Residential
National Park(C)
River, Farmsteads

6. KINGS MEABURN
1969
Rural Main Settlement
Bulk of Settlement
Residential
River, Farmland

7. KIRKBY STEPHEN
1976
Rural Main Settlement,
Pre-industrial Town
Including Bulk of Core
Residential, Other
River

8. MAULDS MEABURN
1969
Rural Other Settlement
Bulk of Settlement
Residential
River, Green, Country House,
Farmland, Park

9. MILBURN
1975
Rural Main Settlement
Bulk of Settlement
Residential, Open Space
A.O.N.B.(23)
Green

10. PENRITH
1981 (1975) Amended
Town (12), Pre-industrial Town
Including Bulk of Core
Residential, Shops/Offices
Castle

South Lakeland

1. AMBLESIDE
1980
Town (6), Pre-industrial Town
Including Bulk of Core
Residential, Shops/Offices, Other
National Park(C)
River, Country House(College),
Park, Mill

2. BEETHAM
1974
Rural Main Settlement
Bulk of Settlement
Residential
A.O.N.B.(1)
River, Country House, Woodland,
Farmstead, Meadows

3. BOWNESS-ON-WINDERMERE
1982
Town (9)
Including Bulk of Core
Residential, Shops/Offices
National Park(C)
Lakeside, Town House, Park

4. BROUGHTON-IN-FURNESS
1982
Rural Other Settlement
Bulk of Settlement
Residential, Open Space, Other

5. BURTON IN KENDAL
1970
Rural Main Settlement,
Pre-industrial Town
Including Part of Core
Residential, Other

6. CARTMEL
1969
Rural Main Settlement,
Pre-industrial Town
Bulk of Settlement
Residential, Open Space, Other
River, Priory, Racecourse,
Farmland, Woodland,
Grammar School

CUMBRIA

7. DENT
1969
Rural Main Settlement,
Pre-industrial Town
Bulk of Settlement
Residential
National Park(H)
River, Meadows

8. GRASMERE (NR. AMBLESIDE)
1984
Urban Village (7)
Including Bulk of Core
Residential, Open Space
National Park(C)
River, Country House

9. GRASMERE, TOWN END
   (NR.AMBLESIDE)
1984
Urban Village (7)
Bulk of Settlement
Residential
National Park(C)
Lakeside, Hotel

10. HEVERSHAM
1970
Rural Main Settlement
Including Bulk of Core
Other

11. KENDAL
1982 (1969) Amended
Town (23), Pre-industrial Town
Including Bulk of Core
Residential, Shops/Offices, Other
River

12. KIRKBY LONSDALE
1969
Rural Main Settlement,
Pre-industrial Town
Including Bulk of Core
Residential, Other
River

13. MILNTHORPE
1970
Rural Main Settlement
Including Part of Core
Other

14. RYDALE (NR. AMBLESIDE)
1984
Urban Village (7)
Bulk of Settlement
Residential
National Park(C)
River, Country House, Park,
Farmstead

15. SEDBERGH
1969
Rural Main Settlement,
Pre-industrial Town
Including Bulk of Core
Residential, Other
National Park(H)

16. STAVELEY
1986
Rural Main Settlement
Including Bulk of Core
Residential, Open Space, Industrial,
Other
National Park(C)
Rivers

17. TROUTBECK (NR. AMBLESIDE)
1981
Urban Village (7)
Bulk of Settlement
Residential
National Park(C)
Farmsteads

18. ULVERSTON
1982 (1971) Amended
Town (12), Pre-industrial Town
Including Bulk of Core
Residential, Shops/Offices, Other
River, Country House(School), Park

DESIGNATION ACTIVITY 1988

Barrow in Furness	8	NORTH VICKERSTOWN
	9	SOUTH VICKERSTOWN
Copeland	8	WHITEHAVEN, TOWN CENTRE (EXTENSION)
South Lakeland	19	HAWKSHEAD (LAKE DISTRICT NATIONAL PARK DESIGNATION)
	20	FAR SAWREY (LAKE DISTRICT NATIONAL PARK DESIGNATION)
	21	NEAR SAWREY (LAKE DISTRICT NATIONAL PARK DESIGNATION)
	15	SEDBERGH (YORKSHIRE DALES NATIONAL PARK DESIGNATION) (EXTENSION)

CUMBRIA

FOOTNOTES

Allerdale

5. COCKERMOUTH, DERWENT AREA — Originally designated as THE GOAT in 1970. Extended in 1976.

Carlisle

2. BURGH BY SANDS — Only that portion of the Conservation Area north of the village street lies within the AONB. The AONB boundary runs parallel to the Roman Wall.

5. CARLISLE, CITY CENTRE — Amalgamating CASTLE (1968), CATHEDRAL (1968) and COURT SQUARE, CARLISLE (1968).

Eden

4. CHURCH BROUGH — Brough is treated as a single settlement with two two nuclei; Church Brough and Market Brough.

South Lakeland

2. BEETHAM — Only that portion of the Conservation Area to the west of the village street occurs within the AONB; the AONB includes Slack Head.

3. BOWNESS-ON-WINDERMERE — Include two centres - BOWNESS and WINDERMERE.

11. KENDAL — Amalgamating STRAMON GATE / KIRKLAND AREA / MARKET PLACE (1969) and THORNY HILLS / CASTLE CRESCENT AREA (1969).

DURHAM

DURHAM

Chester-le-Street

No Conservation Areas

Darlington

1. BISHOPTON
   1972
   Rural Main Settlement
   Bulk of Settlement
   Residential
   Castle, Stream, Green

2. COATHAM MUNDEVILLE
   1980
   Rural Non Settlement
   Not Applicable
   Country House, Park, River, Mill,
   Farmsteads

3. DARLINGTON, COCKERTON
   1968
   Town (85), Pre-industrial Town
   Small Part Excluding Core
   Residential, Other
   Green, Stream

4. DARLINGTON,
   NORTH ROAD STATION
   1972
   Urban Non Settlement (85)
   Not Applicable
   Industrial Monument
   (Railway Station)

5. DARLINGTON, STANHOPE /
   GRANGE ROAD
   1975 (1968) Amalgamated
   Town (85), Pre-industrial Town
   Large Part Excluding Core
   Residential, Open Space

6. DARLINGTON, TOWN CENTRE
   1976
   Town (85), Pre-industrial Town
   Including Bulk of Core
   Residential, Shops/Offices, Other
   Town House(School), Park, River

7. DENTON
   1981
   Rural Main Settlement
   Bulk of Settlement
   Residential
   Farmstead

8. HAUGHTON
   (NR. DARLINGTON)
   1978 (1968) Amended
   Urban Village (85)
   Including Bulk of Core
   Residential, Open Space
   Country House, Park, River

9. HEIGHINGTON
   1972
   Rural Main Settlement
   Including Bulk of Core
   Residential
   Green, Meadow

10. HIGH CONISCLIFFE
    1974
    Rural Main Settlement
    Bulk of Settlement
    Residential
    River, Farmland, Mill, Woodland,
    Stream

11. HURWORTH
    1971
    Rural Main Settlement
    Including Bulk of Core
    Residential
    Country House, Park, River, Green

12. MIDDLETON ONE ROW
    1972
    Rural Main Settlement
    Including Bulk of Core
    Residential, Open Space
    Country House, River, Green

13. PIERCEBRIDGE
    1972
    Rural Main Settlement
    Bulk of Settlement
    Residential
    River, Roman Fort, Green, Meadow,
    Bridge

14. SADBERGE
    1972
    Rural Main Settlement
    Including Bulk of Core
    Residential
    Earthworks(Deserted Village)

15. SUMMERHOUSE
    1978
    Rural Main Settlement
    Bulk of Settlement
    Residential
    Farmland, Farmsteads,
    Earthworks(Deserted Village)

Derwentside

1. BURNOFIELD (NR. STANLEY)
   1984
   Urban Village (41)
   Including Bulk of Core
   Residential, Open Space
   Allotments, Woodland, Streams,
   Country House

2. CONSETT, SHOTLEY BRIDGE
   1981 (1975) Amended
   Town (33)
   Large Part Excluding Core
   Residential, Other
   River, Parkland

3. EBCHESTER (NR. CONSETT)
   1972
   Urban Village (33)
   Including Bulk of Core
   Residential
   Roman Fort, River, Mill, Country
   House, Woodland, Stream

4. ESH
   1975
   Rural Main Settlement
   Including Bulk of Core
   Residential

5. IVESTON (NR. CONSETT)
   1975
   Urban Village (33)
   Bulk of Settlement
   Residential
   Green

6. LANCHESTER
   1972
   Rural Main Settlement
   Including Bulk of Core
   Residential, Other
   River

7. LINTZFORD
   1976
   See Other (41)
   Not Applicable
   Open Space
   River, Meadows, Mill, Farmstead,
   Woodland

8. MEDOMSLEY (NR. CONSETT)
   1975
   Urban Village (33)
   Including Bulk of Core
   Residential
   Farmsteads

DURHAM

9. SATLEY
1975
Rural Main Settlement
Bulk of Settlement
Residential
River, Mill

10. TANFIELD (NR. STANLEY)
1975
Urban Village (41)
Including Bulk of Core
Residential
Country House

Durham

1. BOWBURN
1979
Rural Other Settlement
Including Part of Core
Residential, Open Space
Workers' Housing

2. BRANCEPETH
1981 (1972) Amended
Rural Main Settlement
Bulk of Settlement
Residential, Open Space
Castle, Country House, Park, Ponds, Stream, Farmland

3. BURN HALL (NR. DURHAM)
1981
Urban Non Settlement (26)
Not Applicable
Country House, Park, Rivers, Farmstead, Meadows

4. DURHAM CITY
1980 (1968) Amended
Town (26), Pre-industrial Town
Including Bulk of Core
Residential, Open Space, Shops/ Offices, Other
Ancient Camp, Cathedral Precinct, Castle, River, Woodland, Farmland

5. HALLGARTH
1981
Rural Non Settlement (26)
Not Applicable
Country House

6. HETT
1977
Rural Main Settlement
Bulk of Settlement
Residential
Green, Farmland

7. HOLYWELL
1981
Rural Non Settlement
Not Applicable
Country House, Farmland

8. OLD BRANDON
1976
Urban Village (18)
Bulk of Settlement
Residential
Farmland, Country House

9. OLD CASSOP
1981
Rural Main Settlement
Bulk of Settlement
Residential
Farmsteads, Farmland, River

10. SHADFORTH
1976
Rural Main Settlement
Bulk of Settlement
Residential
Farmland, Woodland

11. SHERBURN
1979
Rural Main Settlement
Including Bulk of Core
Residential
Green

12. SHERBURN HOSPITAL
1981
Urban Non Settlement
Not Applicable
Other
Country House, Park, Farmland, River

13. SHINCLIFFE
1976
Rural Main Settlement
Bulk of Settlement
Residential
River, Farmland

14. SUNDERLAND BRIDGE
1976
Rural Main Settlement
Bulk of Settlement
Residential
River, Meadows, Marshland, Country House, Park, Woodland, Farmland, Lakes, Bridge, Moated Site

Easington

1. CASTLE EDEN
1976
Rural Main Settlement
Bulk of Settlement
Residential, Open Space, Industrial
Country House, Farmland

2. EASINGTON VILLAGE
1974
Rural Main Settlement
Including Bulk of Core
Residential, Open Space
Green

3. HAWTHORN
1974
Rural Main Settlement
Including Bulk of Core
Residential
Farmsteads

Sedgefield

1. AYCLIFFE VILLAGE
1981
Rural Main Settlement
Including Bulk of Core
Residential
Green

2. BISHOP MIDDLEHAM
1982
Rural Main Settlement
Including Bulk of Core
Residential

3. SEDGEFIELD
1971
Rural Main Settlement, Pre-industrial Town
Including Bulk of Core
Residential, Other

Teesdale

1. BARNARD CASTLE
1981 (1969) Amended
Town (5), Pre-industrial Town
Including Bulk of Core
Residential, Open Space, Shops/ Offices
River, Meadows, Castle, Woodland, Country House, Bridge

2. BARNINGHAM
1984
Rural Main Settlement
Bulk of Settlement
Residential
Country House, Park, Pond

DURHAM

3. BOWES
1984
Rural Main Settlement
Bulk of Settlement
Residential
Castle, Roman Fort

4. COTHERSTONE
1984
Rural Main Settlement
Bulk of Settlement
Residential
River, Castle, Park, Mill, Farmland

5. GAINFORD
1971
Rural Main Settlement
Including Bulk of Core
Residential
River, Green

6. HEADLAM
1984
Rural Main Settlement
Bulk of Settlement
Residential
Farmsteads

7. HILTON
1984
Rural Main Settlement
Bulk of Settlement
Residential
Country House, Farmsteads

8. LARTINGTON
1984
Rural Main Settlement
Bulk of Settlement
Residential
Country House, Park

9. MIDDLETON-IN-TEESDALE
1971
Rural Main Settlement
Including Bulk of Core
Residential, Other
River, Meadows, Mills, Country House

10. ROMALDKIRK
1984
Rural Main Settlement
Bulk of Settlement
Residential

11. STAINDROP
1972
Rural Main Settlement,
Pre-industrial Town
Including Bulk of Core
Residential
Green, River, Mill, Woodland

12. WACKERFIELD
1984
Rural Main Settlement
Bulk of Settlement
Residential

13. WHORLTON
1971
Rural Main Settlement
Bulk of Settlement
Residential
Woodland, River, Country Houses, Avenue

Wear Valley

1. BISHOP AUCKLAND
1969
Town (33), Pre-industrial Town
Including Part of Core
Open Space, Shops/Offices
Rivers, Country House, Park, Mill, Woodland

2. CROOK
1975
Twin Town (22)
Including Bulk of Core
Open Space, Shops/Offices
Farmland

3. STANHOPE
1972
Rural Main Settlement
Including Bulk of Core
Residential, Open Space, Other
River, Country Houses, Mill

4. WEST AUCKLAND
(NR BISHOP AUCKLAND)
1975
Urban Village (33)
Bulk of Settlement
Residential, Open Space, Other
River, Green

5. WITTON-LE-WEAR
(NR. CROOK)
1972
Urban Village (22)
Bulk of Settlement
Residential
River, Meadows

6. WOLSINGHAM
1975
Rural Main Settlement,
Pre-industrial Town
Including Bulk of Core
Residential, Open Space, Other
Rivers, Mill

DESIGNATION ACTIVITY 1987

Teesdale

14	CLEATLAM
15	EGGLESTON
16	GRETA BRIDGE
17	INGLETON
18	LANGTON
19	NEWBIGGIN
20	LITTLE NEWSHAM
21	MICKLETON

DURHAM

FOOTNOTES

Darlington

5. DARLINGTON, STANHOPE /
   GRANGE ROAD   Amalgamating STANHOPE GREEN (1968) and HAREWOOD HILL (1968).

Derwentside

7. LINTZFORD   See also Gateshead, TYNE AND WEAR.

HUMBERSIDE

Beverley

1. BEVERLEY
   1984 (1969) Amended
   Town (16), Pre-industrial Town
   Including Bulk of Core
   Residential, Shops/Offices,
   Industrial, Other
   Cathedral Precinct

2. BISHOP BURTON
   1974
   Rural Main Settlement
   Bulk of Settlement
   Residential
   Green, Lake, Farmsteads, Meadow,
   Woodland

3. COTTINGHAM
   1983 (1975) Amended
   Twin Town (54)
   Including Bulk of Core
   Residential, Open Space, Other
   Castle, Town House, Park, Pond

4. HESSLE, SOUTHFIELD
   1979
   Twin Town (54)
   Large Part Excluding Core
   Residential

5. HESSLE, TOWN CENTRE
   1980
   Twin Town (54)
   Including Bulk of Core
   Open Space, Shops/Offices

6. KIRK ELLA (NR. HESSLE)
   1974
   Urban Village (54)
   Including Bulk of Core
   Residential, Other

7. LOCKINGTON
   1980 (1974) Amended
   Rural Main Settlement
   Bulk of Settlement
   Residential
   Stream, Meadows, Castle Mound,
   Farmland

8. NORTH NEWBOLD
   1974
   Rural Main Settlement
   Including Part of Core
   Residential, Other
   Stream, Meadow

9. SOUTH CAVE
   1981 (1974) Amended
   Rural Main Settlement
   Including Bulk of Core
   Residential, Open Space, Other
   Country House, Park, Pond,
   Meadow, Farmstead

10. WALKINGTON
    1974
    Rural Main Settlement
    Including Bulk of Core
    Residential
    Pond, Farmstead

11. WELTON
    1986 (1974) Amended
    Rural Main Settlement
    Including Bulk of Core
    Residential
    Country House, Park, Mill

12. WEST ELLA (NR. HESSLE)
    1974
    Urban Village (54)
    Including Part of Core
    Residential

Boothferry

1. EPWORTH
   1970
   Rural Main Settlement
   Including Part of Core
   Other

2. HOWDEN
   1974
   Rural Main Settlement,
   Pre-industrial Town
   Including Bulk of Core
   Residential, Open Space, Other
   Bishops Palace, Church Precinct,
   Moated Site

3. NORTH CAVE
   1974
   Rural Main Settlement
   Bulk of Settlement
   Residential, Other
   River, Mills, Pond

4. RAWCLIFFE
   1986
   Rural Main Settlement
   Including Part of Core
   Residential, Open Space
   River, Green

5. SNAITH
   1980 (1969) Amended
   Rural Main Settlement,
   Pre-industrial Town
   Including Bulk of Core
   Residential, Other
   Town House

Cleethorpes

1. CLEETHORPES,
   BRADFORD AVENUE
   1976
   Town (36)
   Small Part Excluding Core
   Residential

2. CLEETHORPES,
   CENTRAL SEAFRONT
   1976
   Town (36)
   Including Bulk of Core
   Shops/Offices

3. CLEETHORPES, MILL ROAD
   1976
   Town (36)
   Small Part Excluding Core
   Residential

4. HUMBERSTON
   1976
   Rural Main Settlement
   Including Bulk of Core
   Residential, Open Space
   Farmstead, Meadow

5. LACEBY
   1977
   Rural Main Settlement
   Including Bulk of Core
   Residential

6. LACEBY, COTTAGERS PLOT
   1977
   Rural Main Settlement
   Small Part Excluding Core
   Residential
   Agricultural Community

7. WALTHAM
   1976
   Rural Main Settlement
   Including Bulk of Core
   Residential
   Stream

HUMBERSIDE

East Yorkshire

1. ALLERTHORPE
   1981
   Rural Main Settlement
   Bulk of Settlement
   Residential
   Farmstead

2. BESSINGBY
   (NR. BRIDLINGTON)
   1979
   Urban Village (29)
   Bulk of Settlement
   Residential
   Country House, Park, Farmstead

3. BISHOP WILTON
   1974
   Rural Main Settlement
   Bulk of Settlement
   Residential
   Stream

4. BRIDLINGTON, OLD TOWN
   1982 (1969) Amended
   Town (29), Pre-industrial Town
   Including Bulk of Core
   Residential, Shops/Offices, Other

5. BURTON AGNES
   1974
   Rural Main Settlement
   Including Bulk of Core
   Residential, Open Space
   Country House, Formal Garden,
   Lake, Stream

6. CRANSWICK
   1976
   Rural Other Settlement
   Including Bulk of Core
   Residential, Open Space
   Green

7. DRIFFIELD (NORTH)
   1984 (1980) Amended
   Town (9)
   Including Part of Core
   Residential, Open Space, Shops/
   Offices
   Earthworks, Town House, Park,
   Pond

8. DRIFFIELD (SOUTH)
   1980
   Town (9)
   Large Part Excluding Core
   Residential, Industrial
   Canal Basin, Mill-stream, Mill

9. FLAMBOROUGH
   1974
   Rural Main Settlement
   Including Bulk of Core
   Residential, Open Space, Other
   Castle, Farmsteads

10. GOODMANHAM
    1978
    Rural Main Settlement
    Bulk of Settlement
    Residential
    Farmland, Meadows, Farmstead

11. HUTTON
    1977
    Rural Main Settlement
    Including Bulk of Core
    Residential
    Windmill

12. KILHAM
    1976
    Rural Main Settlement,
    Pre-industrial Town
    Bulk of Settlement
    Residential
    Farmsteads

13. LONDESBOROUGH
    1977
    Rural Main Settlement
    Bulk of Settlement
    Residential
    Country House, Park, Lake

14. MARKET WEIGHTON
    1980 (1974) Amended
    Rural Main Settlement,
    Pre-industrial Town
    Including Part of Core
    Residential, Industrial, Other

15. NAFFERTON
    1981
    Rural Main Settlement
    Including Bulk of Core
    Residential, Open Space, Other
    Country House, Park, Lake,
    Meadow, Moated Site

16. NORTH DALTON
    1978
    Rural Main Settlement
    Bulk of Settlement
    Residential
    Farmland, Farmsteads, Pond

17. POCKLINGTON
    1974
    Rural Main Settlement,
    Pre-industrial Town
    Including Bulk of Core
    Residential, Other
    School, Stream

18. SEWERBY (NR. BRIDLINGTON)
    1972
    Urban Village (29)
    Including Bulk of Core
    Residential
    Farmstead

19. SLEDMERE
    1974
    Rural Main Settlement
    Bulk of Settlement
    Residential
    Country House, Park

20. STAMFORD BRIDGE
    1976
    Rural Main Settlement
    Including Bulk of Core
    Residential
    River, Mill

21. WARTER
    1978
    Rural Main Settlement
    Bulk of Settlement
    Residential
    Priory

22. WETWANG
    1978
    Rural Main Settlement
    Including Bulk of Core
    Residential

Glanford

1. ALKBOROUGH
   1979 (1970) Amended
   Rural Main Settlement
   Including Bulk of Core
   Residential
   Country House, Park, Earthwork

2. APPLEBY
   1973
   Rural Main Settlement
   Bulk of Settlement
   Residential
   Stream, Meadow, Woodland

3. BARROW UPON HUMBER
   1986 (1975) Amended
   Rural Main Settlement
   Including Bulk of Core
   Residential, Other

HUMBERSIDE

4. BARTON UPON HUMBER
1982 (1973) Amended
Town (8), Pre-industrial Town
Including Bulk of Core
Residential, Open Space, Shops/Offices

5. BRIGG
1971
Town (5), Pre-industrial Town
Including Part of Core
Shops/Offices
River

6. BURTON UPON STATHER
1970
Rural Main Settlement
Including Bulk of Core
Residential, Other

7. KIRTON IN LINDSEY
1985 (1971) Amended
Rural Main Settlement,
Pre-industrial Town
Including Part of Core
Residential, Open Space, Other

8. KIRTON, ST. ANDREWS
1985
Rural Main Settlement,
Pre-industrial Town
Including Part of Core
Other

9. NORMANBY
1985
Rural Other Settlement
Bulk of Settlement
Residential
Country House, Park, Pond

10. REDBOURNE
1985
Rural Main Settlement
Including Bulk of Core
Residential
Castle, Farmstead

11. SAXBY ALL SAINTS
1977
Rural Main Settlement
Bulk of Settlement
Residential
Woodland, Country House,
Park, Meadows, Moated Site

12. SCAWBY
1985
Rural Main Settlement
Including Bulk of Core
Residential
Country Houses

13. WINTERINGHAM
1985
Rural Main Settlement
Including Bulk of Core
Residential

14. WINTERTON
1985
Rural Main Settlement
Including Part of Core
Residential
Park

Great Grimsby

1. GREAT COATES (NR. GRIMSBY)
1972
Urban Village (92)
Including Bulk of Core
Residential
Country House, Farmsteads,
Meadows, Moated Site

2. GRIMSBY, OLD CLEE
1984 (1970) Amended
Town (92), Pre-industrial Town
Small Part Excluding Core
Residential, Open Space
Farmstead, Meadows, Moated Site

3. SCARTHO
1973
Town (92), Pre-industrial Town
Small Part Excluding Core
Residential

4. WELLOW
1973
Town (92), Pre-industrial Town
Large Part Excluding Core
Residential, Open Space

Holderness

1. ALDBROUGH
1976 (1974) Amended
Rural Main Settlement
Including Bulk of Core
Residential, Other
Country House, Park

2. BRANDESBURTON
1977
Rural Main Settlement
Including Bulk of Core
Residential

3. BURTON PIDSEA
1976 (1974) Amended
Rural Main Settlement
Including Bulk of Core
Residential
Farmstead, Windmill,
Country House

4. EASINGTON
1974
Rural Main Settlement
Including Bulk of Core
Residential, Other
Farmsteads

5. HEDON
1976 (1969) Amended
Town (5), Pre-industrial Town
Including Bulk of Core
Residential, Shops/Offices
Farmland

6. HORNSEA
1976 (1969) Amended
Town (7)
Including Bulk of Core
Residential, Open Space, Shops/Offices
Lakeside, Moated Site

7. PATRINGTON
1976 (1969) Amended
Rural Main Settlement,
Pre-industrial Town
Including Bulk of Core
Residential, Open Space, Other

8. SIGGLESTHORNE
1986
Rural Main Settlement
Including Bulk of Core
Residential
Country House, Park

Kingston upon Hull

1. ALBION / JARRATT STREET
1975
Town (268), Pre-industrial Town
Including Part of Core
Residential, Shops/Offices,
Industrial

2. CHARTERHOUSE
1970
Town (268), Pre-industrial Town
Including Part of Core
Other
Almshouses

3. GARDEN VILLAGE
1970
Town (268), Pre-industrial Town
Small Part Excluding Core
Residential
Planned Community

HUMBERSIDE

4. OLD TOWN
1981 (1973) Amended
Town (268), Pre-industrial Town
Including Part of Core
Shops/Offices, Industrial
River, Docks

5. SUTTON
1975
Town (268), Pre-industrial Town
Small Part Excluding Core
Residential, Other

6. THE AVENUES
1974
Town (268), Pre-industrial Town
Large Part Excluding Core
Residential, Open Space

Scunthorpe

1. NEW FRODINGHAM
1986
Town (66)
Small Part Excluding Core
Residential

2. OLD CROSBY VILLAGE
1976
Town (66)
Small Part Excluding Core
Residential

DESIGNATION ACTIVITY 1987

East Yorkshire   23   EVERINGHAM

Holderness   9   SPROATLEY

DESIGNATION ACTIVITY 1988

Beverley   13   ELLOUGHTON

FOOTNOTES

Beverley

9. SOUTH CAVE   The designated area includes a detached portion at Pinfold, West End.

Boothferry

5. SNAITH   The 1980 amendment reduced the area previously designated.

Holderness

3. BURTON PIDSEA   The designated area comprises two portions, one centred on the parish church and the other on Green Lane and the mill.

LANCASHIRE

LANCASHIRE

Blackburn

1. CHAPELTOWN
   (NR. EDGWORTH)
   1970
   Urban Village (3)
   Bulk of Settlement
   Residential, Other

2. CORPORATION PARK
   1974
   Town (88), Pre-industrial Town
   Large Part Excluding Core
   Residential, Open Space

3. EDGWORTH
   1972
   Town (3)
   Including Bulk of Core
   Residential, Open Space, Other

4. HODDLESDEN (NR. DARWEN)
   1975
   Urban Village (30)
   Including Bulk of Core
   Residential

5. REVIDGE, DUKES BROW
   1975
   Town (88), Pre-industrial Town
   Small Part Excluding Core
   Residential

6. RICHMOND TERRACE /
   ST. JOHNS
   1975
   Town (88), Pre-industrial Town
   Including Part of Core
   Residential, Shops/Offices

7. WITTON, GRIFFIN LODGE
   1975
   Town (88), Pre-industrial Town
   Small Part Excluding Core
   Residential, Open Space

Blackpool

1. STANLEY PARK
   1984
   Town (148)
   Large Part Excluding Core
   Residential, Open Space

2. TALBOT SQUARE
   1984
   Town (148)
   Including Part of Core
   Shops/Offices
   Pier, Seafront

Burnley

1. BURNLEY WOOD
   1985
   Town (70), Pre-industrial Town
   Large Part Excluding Core
   Residential

2. HARLE SYKE
   1986 (1977) Amended
   Rural Other Settlement
   Including Part of Core
   Residential, Industrial
   Industrial Mill

3. HURSTWOOD
   1973
   Rural Other Settlement
   Bulk of Settlement
   Residential
   Country House, Park, Stream

4. JIB HILL
   1971
   Town (70), Pre-industrial Town
   Small Part Excluding Core
   Residential

5. PADIHAM
   1984 (1975) Amended
   Town (9)
   Including Part of Core
   Residential, Open Space, Shops/
   Offices
   River

6. PALATINE
   1977
   Town (70), Pre-industrial Town
   Small Part Excluding Core
   Residential

7. WORSTHORNE
   1978
   Rural Main Settlement
   Including Bulk of Core
   Residential, Industrial, Other

Chorley

1. ABBEY VILLAGE
   (NR. WITHNELL)
   1974
   Town (3)
   Bulk of Settlement
   Residential, Industrial
   Industrial Mill

2. CROSTON
   1969
   Rural Main Settlement
   Including Part of Core
   Residential
   River, Park, Woodland, Mill,
   Country House, Avenue, Meadows

3. ST. GEORGES
   1985
   Town (35), Pre-industrial Town
   Including Part of Core
   Residential, Other

4. ST. LAURENCES
   1985
   Town (35), Pre-industrial Town
   Including Part of Core
   Other

5. WITHNELL FOLD
   (NR. WITHNELL)
   1969
   Urban Village (3)
   Bulk of Settlement
   Residential, Open Space, Industrial
   Canal, Farmland, Country House,
   Park, Woodland, Industrial Mills,
   Reservoir

Fylde

1. KIRKHAM
   1974
   Town (6), Pre-industrial Town
   Including Bulk of Core
   Residential, Shops/Offices

2. LYTHAM
   1980 (1975) Amended
   Town (40)
   Including Bulk of Core
   Residential, Open Space, Shops/
   Offices, Other
   Seafront, Green

3. LYTHAM ST. ANNES, PORRITT
   HOUSES
   1986
   Town (40)
   Small Part Excluding Core
   Residential, Open Space
   Seafront

4. SINGLETON
   1979 (1975) Amended
   Rural Main Settlement
   Bulk of Settlement
   Residential
   Farmsteads, Farmland

LANCASHIRE

5. THISTLETON
1975
Rural Other Settlement
Bulk of Settlement
Residential
Farmsteads

6. WREA GREEN
1975
Rural Other Settlement
Including Bulk of Core
Residential, Open Space
Green, Pond

Hyndburn

1. ACCRINGTON, CHRIST CHURCH
1976
Town (36)
Large Part Excluding Core
Residential, Other

2. ACRINGTON, TOWN CENTRE
1976
Town (36)
Including Bulk of Core
Residential, Shops/Offices

3. ALTHAM
1976
Rural Main Settlement
Bulk of Settlement
Residential, Other
River, Meadow

4. CLAYTON LE MOORS, MERCER PARK
1976
Town (6)
Large Part Excluding Core
Residential, Open Space

5. GREAT HARWOOD, TOWN CENTRE
1976
Town (11), Pre-industrial Town
Including Part of Core
Residential, Shops/Offices

6. STANHILL
(NR. OSWALDTWISTLE)
1976
Urban Village (15)
Including Part of Core
Residential

7. TOTTLEWORTH (NR. RISHTON)
1976
Urban Village (6)
Bulk of Settlement
Residential
Stream

Lancaster

1. ARKHOLME
1981
Rural Main Settlement
Bulk of Settlement
Residential
Country House

2. BOLTON-LE-SANDS
1981
Rural Main Settlement
Including Bulk of Core
Residential
Canal

3. BORWICK
1974
Rural Main Settlement
Bulk of Settlement
Residential
Country House, Canal

4. BROOKHOUSE
1981
Rural Other Settlement
Including Bulk of Core
Residential, Other
A.O.N.B.(12)
River

5. CANTSFIELD
1981
Rural Main Settlement
Bulk of Settlement
Residential
Farmsteads

6. DOLPHINHOLME
1977
Rural Other Settlement
Bulk of Settlement
Residential
River, Meadows, Woodland

7. GLASSON DOCK
1977
Rural Other Settlement
Bulk of Settlement
Residential, Industrial
River, Dock/Basin, Canal

8. GRESSINGHAM
1981
Rural Main Settlement
Bulk of Settlement
Residential
A.O.N.B.(12)
Stream, Farmsteads

9. HALTON
1981
Rural Main Settlement
Including Bulk of Core
Residential
River, Country House, Castle Mound

10. HORNBY
1973
Rural Main Settlement,
Pre-industrial Town
Including Bulk of Core
Residential
A.O.N.B.(12)
Country House, Park, River, Bridge

11. IREBY
1981
Rural Main Settlement
Bulk of Settlement
Residential
Farmstead, Stream

12. LANCASTER, BATH MILL
1983
Town (46), Pre-industrial Town
Small Part Excluding Core
Residential
Canal

13. LANCASTER, CASTLE PRECINCT
1969
Town (46), Pre-industrial Town
Including Part of Core
Residential, Shops/Offices
Castle

14. LANCASTER, DALTON SQUARE
1977
Town (46), Pre-industrial Town
Including Part of Core
Residential, Shops/Offices

15. LANCASTER, HIGH STREET
1977
Town (46), Pre-industrial Town
Including Part of Core
Residential, Shops/Offices

16. LANCASTER, MARKET SQUARE
1970
Town (46), Pre-industrial Town
Including Part of Core
Shops/Offices

LANCASHIRE

17. LANCASTER,
ST. GEORGES QUAY
1972
Town (46), Pre-industrial Town
Including Part of Core
Residential, Open Space, Industrial
Industrial Monument(Warehouses),
River Estuary, Quay

18. LANCASTER, WESTFIELD WAR
MEMORIAL VILLAGE
1986
Town (46), Pre-industrial Town
Small Part Excluding Core
Residential

19. LANCASTER, WILLIAMSON
PARK
1986
Town (46), Pre-industrial Town
Large Part Excluding Core
Open Space

20. MELLING
1981
Rural Main Settlement
Bulk of Settlement
Residential, Open Space
Farmstead, Green, Meadow

21. MORECAMBE, HEYSHAM
VILLAGE
1972
Town (41)
Including Part of Core
Residential, Open Space, Shops/
Offices
Seafront, Marsh

22. NETHER BURROW
1981
Rural Main Settlement
Bulk of Settlement
Residential
Stream

23. NETHER KELLET
1981
Rural Main Settlement
Bulk of Settlement
Residential, Open Space
Tithe Barn, Farmstead

24. OVER KELLET
1973
Rural Main Settlement
Including Bulk of Core
Residential
Country House, Green, Farmstead

25. OVERTON
1981
Rural Main Settlement
Including Bulk of Core
Residential
Sea Inlet

26. PRIEST HUTTON
1974
Rural Main Settlement
Bulk of Settlement
Residential

27. SLYNE WITH HEST
1981
Rural Main Settlement
Including Bulk of Core
Residential, Other

28. SUNDERLAND POINT
1981
Rural Non Settlement
Not Applicable
Farmland, River, Sea Inlet, Seafront

29. TUNSTALL
1981
Rural Main Settlement
Bulk of Settlement
Residential
Country House, Farmsteads

30. WARTON
1973
Rural Main Settlement
Including Bulk of Core
Residential
A.O.N.B.(1)

31. WENNINGTON
1981
Rural Main Settlement
Bulk of Settlement
Residential, Other
Country House(School), Park, River,
Green

32. WHITTINGTON
1981
Rural Main Settlement
Bulk of Settlement
Residential
Country House, Park, Farmstead,
Stream, Meadow

33. WRAY
1973
Rural Main Settlement
Bulk of Settlement
Residential
A.O.N.B.(12)
River, Bridge, Woodland, Meadow

34. WRAYTON
1981
Rural Other Settlement
Bulk of Settlement
Residential
Farmsteads

35. YEALAND COWYERS /
REDMAYNE
1981
Rural Main Settlements
Bulk of Settlements
Residential
A.O.N.B.(1)
Farmland, Woodland, Country
House

Pendle

1. BARROWFORD, HIGHERFORD
1981
Town (5)
Large Part Excluding Core
Residential, Industrial
River

2. CARR HALL
(NR. BARROWFORD)
1984
Urban Village (5)
Including Part of Core
Residential
Farmland, Woodland, Stream,
Farmsteads

3. CARR HALL ROAD
(NR. BARROWFORD)
1984
Urban Village (5)
Including Part of Core
Residential
Farmland

4. COLNE, ALBERT ROAD
1984
Town (18)
Including Part of Core
Residential, Shops/Offices

5. HIGHAM
1981
Rural Main Settlement
Including Bulk of Core
Residential

6. WYCOLLER (NR. TRAWDEN)
1972
Urban Village (2)
Bulk of Settlement
Residential
River, Bridges, Country House

LANCASHIRE

Preston

1. AVENHAM
   1978 (1976) Amended
   Town (87), Pre-industrial Town
   Large Part Excluding Core
   Residential, Open Space, Other
   River

2. FULWOOD,
   HARRIS CHILDRENS HOME
   1984
   Town (24)
   Small Part Excluding Core
   Other

3. FULWOOD,
   WATLING STREET ROAD
   1975
   Town (24)
   Large Part Excluding Core
   Residential, Open Space

4. INGLEWHITE
   1986
   Rural Other Settlement
   Bulk of Settlement
   Stream, Farmland, Farmsteads

5. PRESTON, ASHTON
   1984
   Town (87), Pre-industrial Town
   Large Part Excluding Core
   Residential

6. PRESTON, DEEPDALE
   ENCLOSURE
   1986
   Town (87), Pre-industrial Town
   Small Part Excluding Core
   Residential, Open Space

7. PRESTON, MARKET SQUARE
   1984
   Town (87), Pre-industrial Town
   Including Part of Core
   Shops/Offices

8. PRESTON, ST IGNATIUS
   SQUARE
   1982
   Town (87), Pre-industrial Town
   Small Part Excluding Core
   Residential, Other

9. PRESTON, ST. AUGUSTINES
   1986
   Town (87), Pre-industrial Town
   Small Part Excluding Core
   Residential, Other

10. PRESTON, WINKLEY SQUARE
    1984 (1976) Amended
    Town (87), Pre-industrial Town
    Including Part of Core
    Open Space, Shops/Offices, Other

Ribble Valley

1. BOLTON-BY-BOWLAND
   1974
   Rural Main Settlement
   Bulk of Settlement
   Residential
   A.O.N.B.(12)
   Stream

2. CHATBURN
   1974
   Rural Main Settlement
   Including Part of Core
   Residential, Open Space
   Stream

3. CHIPPING
   1969
   Rural Main Settlement
   Including Bulk of Core
   Residential, Other
   A.O.N.B.(12)
   Stream

4. CLITHEROE
   1979 (1973) Amended
   Town (14), Pre-industrial Town
   Including Bulk of Core
   Residential, Open Space, Shops/
   Offices, Other
   Castle

5. DOWNHAM
   1978
   Rural Main Settlement
   Bulk of Settlement
   Residential
   A.O.N.B.(12)
   Country House, Meadows, Park,
   Stream, Farmstead

6. GISBURN
   1974
   Rural Main Settlement
   Bulk of Settlement
   Residential

7. GRINDLETON
   1974
   Rural Main Settlement
   Bulk of Settlement
   Residential
   A.O.N.B.(12)

8. LONGRIDGE
   1979
   Town (7)
   Including Bulk of Core
   Residential, Shops/Offices, Other

9. NEWTON
   1974
   Rural Main Settlement
   Bulk of Settlement
   Residential
   A.O.N.B.(12)
   Farmland, River

10. PENDLETON
    1969
    Rural Main Settlement
    Bulk of Settlement
    Residential
    Stream

11. RIBCHESTER
    1973
    Rural Main Settlement
    Including Bulk of Core
    Residential, Open Space
    Country House, River, Roman Fort,
    Stream, Meadows

12. SAWLEY
    1978 (1971) Amended
    Rural Main Settlement
    Bulk of Settlement
    Residential
    A.O.N.B.(12)
    Abbey, River, Meadows

13. SLAIDBURN
    1974
    Rural Main Settlement
    Bulk of Settlement
    Residential
    A.O.N.B.(12)
    River, Meadows

14. WADDINGTON
    1974
    Rural Main Settlement
    Bulk of Settlement
    Residential
    A.O.N.B.(12)
    Stream, Country House

15. WHALLEY
    1972
    Rural Main Settlement
    Including Bulk of Core
    Residential, Other
    A.O.N.B.(12)
    Abbey, River, Bridge

LANCASHIRE

16. WISWELL
1972
Rural Main Settlement
Including Bulk of Core
Residential
A.O.N.B.(12)

Rossendale

1. BACUP, TOWN CENTRE
1982
Town (15)
Including Bulk of Core
Residential, Shops/Offices

2. CHATTERTON / STRONGSTRY
1974
Urban Village (3)
Bulk of Settlement
Residential, Open Space
River, Meadows

3. CLOUGHFOLD
(NR. RAWTENSTALL)
1974
Urban Village (22)
Including Bulk of Core
Residential

4. GOODSHAW FOLD
(NR. RAWTENSTALL)
1978
Urban Village (22)
Bulk of Settlement
Residential
Stream

5. IRWELL VALE
(NR. HASLINGDEN)
1974
Urban Village (16)
Bulk of Settlement
Residential, Industrial
Industrial Mill, River

6. WHITWORTH, WHITWORTH
SQUARE
1974
Town (8)
Including Bulk of Core
Residential, Other

South Ribble

1. BAMBER BRIDGE, CHURCH
ROAD (NR. WALTON-LE-DALE)
1985
Urban Village (29)
Including Part of Core
Residential, Other

2. LEYLAND, LEYLAND CROSS
1978
Town (27)
Including Part of Core
Residential, Shops/Offices

3. WALTON-LE-DALE, CHURCH
BROW
1985
Town (29), Pre-industrial Town
Including Part of Core
Other
River

4. WALTON-LE-DALE, WALTON
GREEN
1976
Town (29), Pre-industrial Town
Small Part Excluding Core
Residential
River

West Lancashire

1. APPLEY BRIDGE, ASHFIELD
TERRACE
1975
Rural Other Settlement
Large Part Excluding Core
Residential

2. AUGHTON, ST. MICHAELS
CHURCH
1975
Rural Main Settlement
Bulk of Settlement
Residential
Country House

3. AUGHTON, WEST TOWER
1975
Rural Non Settlement
Not Applicable
Country House, Meadows

4. BISPHAM GREEN
1975
Rural Main Settlement
Bulk of Settlement
Residential
Farmstead

5. BISPHAM, MALT KILN LANE /
CHORLEY ROAD
1975
Rural Other Settlement
Including Part of Core
Residential

6. BRIARS BROOK
(NR. ORMSKIRK)
1985
Urban Village (28)
Bulk of Settlement
Residential
Country House(Hotel), Park, River,
Mill

7. BURSCOUGH BRIDGE,
JUNCTION LANE
1982
Urban Village (28)
Small Part Excluding Core
Residential

8. BURSCOUGH, TOP LOCKS
1975
Urban Non Settlement (28)
Not Applicable
Canal(Locks)

9. GRANVILLE PARK
1975
Rural Other Settlement
Large Part Excluding Core
Residential

10. GREAT ALTCAR
1985
Rural Main Settlement
Bulk of Settlement
Residential
Farmsteads

11. HALSALL VILLAGE
1975
Rural Main Settlement
Including Bulk of Core
Residential, Open Space
Country House, Park, Meadows

12. HOLT GREEN
1985 (1975) Amended
Rural Other Settlement
Including Bulk of Core
Residential
Woodland

13. LATHOM PARK
(NR. ORMSKIRK)
1985
Urban Village (28)
Bulk of Settlement
Residential
Country House, Park, Farmstead

14. NEWBURGH (NR. ORMSKIRK)
1985 (1972) Amended
Urban Village (28)
Including Bulk of Core
Residential, Other

LANCASHIRE

15. ORMSKIRK, RUFF LANE
1985 (1975) Amended
Town (28), Pre-industrial Town
Large Part Excluding Core
Residential

16. ORMSKIRK, TOWN CENTRE
1985 (1975) Amended
Town (28), Pre-industrial Town
Including Bulk of Core
Residential, Shops/Offices, Other

17. PARBOLD, LANCASTER LANE
1985 (1975) Amended
Rural Main Settlement
Large Part Excluding Core
Residential, Other
Country Houses, Farmsteads

18. PARBOLD, MILL LANE
1985 (1975) Amended
Rural Main Settlement
Including Part of Core
Residential, Industrial
Canal, Windmill, Canal Wharf

19. PINFOLD
1975
Rural Other Settlement
Bulk of Settlement
Residential
Canal

20. ROBY MILL
(NR. UP HOLLAND)
1975
Urban Village (43)
Bulk of Settlement
Residential
Cemetary, Ponds

21. RUFFORD
1975
Rural Main Settlement
Including Bulk of Core
Residential
Country Houses, Park, Canal

22. SCARISBRICK HALL
1975
Rural Non Settlement
Not Applicable
Country House, Park, Woodland,
Canal, Lake

23. SOLLOM
1975
Rural Non Settlement
Not Applicable
Farmsteads

24. TARLETON, FULWOOD
AVENUE / DOUGLAS AVENUE
1975
Rural Main Settlement
Small Part Excluding Core
Residential

25. UP HOLLAND
1975
Twin Town (43),
 Pre-industrial Town
Including Bulk of Core
Residential, Shops/Offices

26. UP HOLLAND, GARNET LEAS
1985
Twin Town (43),
Pre-industrial Town
Small Part Excluding Core
Residential

Wyre

1. CALDER VALE
1974
Rural Other Settlement
Including Bulk of Core
Residential, Industrial
A.O.N.B.(12)
Industrial Mill, River

2. CHURCHTOWN
1973
Rural Main Settlement
Bulk of Settlement
Residential, Other
River

3. FLEETWOOD, ALBERT
SQUARE
1982
Town (28)
Including Part of Core
Residential, Shops/Offices

4. FLEETWOOD, PHAROS
1982
Town (28)
Including Part of Core
Residential, Open Space, Other
River Estuary

5. FLEETWOOD, THE MOUNT
1982
Town (28)
Including Part of Core
Residential, Open Space

6. GARSTANG
1972
Rural Main Settlement,
Pre-industrial Town
Including Bulk of Core
Residential, Other
River, Canal, Meadow, Bridge

7. POULTON-LE-FYLDE
1975
Town (18)
Including Bulk of Core
Residential, Shops/Offices

8. SCORTON
1972
Rural Main Settlement
Including Bulk of Core
Residential, Open Space, Other
Stream

DESIGNATION ACTIVITY 1987

Lancaster   36 MOOR LANE MILLS

Pendle   1 BARROWFORD   (EXTENSION)

Preston   10 WINKLEY SQUARE   (EXTENSION)

Rossendale   7 LOVECLOUGH FOLD (NR RAWTENSTALL)

LANCASHIRE

FOOTNOTES

Fylde

2. LYTHAM — The town has two nuclei (LYTHAM and ST ANNES). Details as to scale of coverage which refer to the core relate to the relevant nucleus.

Lancaster

6. DOLPHINHOLME — This Conservation Area extends into Wyre, LANCASHIRE.

21. MORECAMBE, HEYSHAM VILLAGE — The town has two nuclei (MORECOMBE and HEYSHAM). Details as to scale of coverage which refer to the core relate to the relevant nucleus.

Wyre

8. SCORTON — This is the main settlement of Nether Wyresdale Civil Parish.

NORTHUMBERLAND

Alnwick

1. ALNMOUTH
1972
Rural Main Settlement,
Pre-industrial Town
Bulk of Settlement
Residential, Open Space, Other
A.O.N.B.(25)
River Estuary, Sea Inlet, Meadows

2. ALNWICK
1977 (1972) Amended
Town (7), Pre-industrial Town
Including Bulk of Core
Residential, Shops/Offices
Castle

3. EGLINGHAM
1976
Rural Main Settlement
Bulk of Settlement
Residential, Open Space
Farmland, Stream, Country House,
Farmstead

4. FELTON
1985
Rural Main Settlement
Including Bulk of Core
Residential
River, Bridge, Mill, Stream, Park

5. GLANTON
1984
Rural Main Settlement
Bulk of Settlement
Residential

6. NEWTON-ON-THE-MOOR
1985
Rural Main Settlement
Bulk of Settlement
Residential
Heath

7. ROTHBURY
1972
Rural Main Settlement
Including Bulk of Core
Residential, Other
Green, River

8. WARKWORTH
1972
Rural Main Settlement,
Pre-industrial Town
Bulk of Settlement
Residential, Open Space, Other
Castle, River, Bridge, Woodland

9. WHITTINGHAM
1976
Rural Main Settlement
Bulk of Settlement
Residential
River, Meadows

Berwick upon Tweed

1. BAMBURGH
1972
Rural Main Settlement,
Pre-industrial Town
Including Bulk of Core
Residential, Open Space, Other
A.O.N.B.(25)
Castle, Cliffs, Seafront, Green

2. BERWICK UPON TWEED
1970
Town (12), Pre-industrial Town
Including Bulk of Core
Residential, Shops/Offices
Town Wall, River Estuary

3. HOLY ISLAND
1972
Rural Main Settlement
Bulk of Settlement
Residential, Open Space
A.O.N.B.(25)
Priory, Farmland, Sea-girt Island,
Golf Course, Cliffs, Country House

4. NORHAM
1984
Rural Main Settlement,
Pre-industrial Town
Bulk of Settlement
Residential
River, Castle, Meadows

Blyth Valley

1. BLYTH, BONDICAR TERRACE
1979
Town (36)
Including Part of Core
Residential, Other

2. BLYTH, CENTRAL
1979
Town (36)
Including Part of Core
Shops/Offices, Other

3. BLYTH, HERITAGE
1979
Town (36)
Including Part of Core
Residential, Shops/Offices, Other

4. CRAMLINGTON VILLAGE
(NR. SEATON DELAVAL)
1975
Urban Village (34)
Including Bulk of Core
Residential, Open Space, Other
Country House, Park

5. HOLYWELL
(NR. SEATON DELAVAL)
1977
Urban Village (34)
Including Bulk of Core
Residential
River, Meadows, Woodland,
Farmstead

Castle Morpeth

1. CAMBO
1975
Rural Main Settlement
Bulk of Settlement
Residential

2. LONGHIRST
1980
Rural Main Settlement
Bulk of Settlement
Residential
Country House, Park,
Country House(School), Stream

3. MATFEN
1973
Rural Main Settlement
Bulk of Settlement
Residential, Other
Green, River

4. MORPETH
1970
Town (15), Pre-industrial Town
Including Bulk of Core
Residential, Shops/Offices
River

5. NETHERWITTON
1985
Rural Main Settlement
Bulk of Settlement
Residential
River, Woodland, Country House,
Park

6. PONTELAND
1973
Rural Main Settlement
Including Bulk of Core
Residential, Other
River

NORTHUMBERLAND

7. STAMFORDHAM
1975
Rural Main Settlement
Including Bulk of Core
Residential
Green, Stream, Country House, Park

8. WHALTON
1973
Rural Main Settlement
Bulk of Settlement
Residential
Meadow

Tynedale

1. ALLENDALE TOWN
1972
Rural Main Settlement
Bulk of Settlement
Residential, Other
A.O.N.B.(23)
River, Mill, Woodland

2. BLANCHLAND
1972
Rural Main Settlement
Bulk of Settlement
Residential
A.O.N.B.(23)
Abbey, River, Stream

3. CORBRIDGE
1974
Rural Main Settlement,
Pre-industrial Town
Including Bulk of Core
Residential, Other
River, Town House

4. HEXHAM
1972
Town (10), Pre-industrial Town
Including Bulk of Core
Residential, Open Space, Shops/Offices
Priory

5. HUMSHAUGH
1975
Rural Main Settlement
Bulk of Settlement
Residential
Country House, Woodland, Farmsteads

6. OVINGHAM
1972
Rural Main Settlement
Including Bulk of Core
Residential
River, Stream, Meadows

Wansbeck

1. BEDLINGTON
1971
Town (27)
Including Bulk of Core
Residential, Shops/Offices

2. BOTHAL VILLAGE
(NR.ASHINGTON)
1986
Urban Village (24)
Bulk of Settlement
Residential
River, Stream, Castle, Woodland

3. NEWBIGGIN BY SEA
1986
Town (12), Pre-industrial Town
Large Part Excluding Core
Residential
Seafront

DESIGNATION ACTIVITY 1987

Berwick upon Tweed 5 BELFORD

DESIGNATION ACTIVITY 1988

Berwick upon Tweed 2 BERWICK UPON TWEED (EXTENSION)

Castle Morpeth
9 BELSAY
10 CAPHEATON
11 HIGH CALTERTON
12 MIDDLETON
13 LONGHORSLEY
14 WEST THURSTON
6 PONTELAND (EXTENSION)

FOOTNOTE

Castle Morpeth

1. CAMBO The village comprises the main settlement of Wallington Demesne Civil Parish.

NORTH YORKSHIRE

Craven

1. APPLETREEWICK
1969
Rural Main Settlement
Bulk of Settlement
Residential
National Park(H)

2. ARNCLIFFE
1978
Rural Main Settlement
Bulk of Settlement
Residential
National Park(H)
River

3. BOLTON ABBEY
1969
Rural Main Settlement
Bulk of Settlement
Residential, Open Space
National Park(H)
Abbey, Country House, Park, River,
Tithe Barn

4. BRADLEY
1970
Rural Main Settlement
Including Bulk of Core
Residential, Open Space, Industrial
Stream, Meadows

5. BUCKDEN
1969
Rural Main Settlement
Bulk of Settlement
Residential
National Park(H)
Country House, Stream

6. BURNSALL
1969
Rural Main Settlement
Bulk of Settlement
Residential
National Park(H)
River

7. BURTON IN LONSDALE
1978
Rural Main Settlement
Including Bulk of Core
Residential
Castle Mound

8. CARLETON
1979
Rural Main Settlement
Including Bulk of Core
Residential, Industrial
Stream, Almshouses

9. CLAPHAM
1978
Rural Main Settlement
Bulk of Settlement
Residential
National Park(H)
Green, River, Woodland

10. CONISTON COLD
1979
Rural Main Settlement
Bulk of Settlement
Residential
Meadows, Stream

11. CONONLEY
1986 (1980) Amended
Rural Main Settlement
Including Bulk of Core
Residential, Open Space
River, Meadows

12. DRAUGHTON
1981
Rural Main Settlement
Bulk of Settlement
Residential
Stream, Meadows

13. EAST MARTON
1979
Rural Main Settlement
Bulk of Settlement
Residential
Canal, Meadows

14. EASTBY
1986
Rural Main Settlement
Bulk of Settlement
Residential
National Park(H)
Farmstead, Farmland, Woodland

15. EMBSAY
1986
Rural Main Settlement
Including Bulk of Core
Residential
National Park(H)
Farmstead, Farmland

16. FARNHILL
1980
Rural Main Settlement
Bulk of Settlement
Residential, Open Space, Industrial
Canal, Country House, Farmland

17. GARGRAVE
1980
Rural Main Settlement
Including Bulk of Core
Residential, Open Space, Other
Canal, River, Stream, Meadows,
Green, Moated Site

18. GIGGLESWICK
1978
Rural Main Settlement
Including Bulk of Core
Residential, Open Space, Other
River

19. GRASSINGTON
1969
Rural Main Settlement
Including Part of Core
Residential, Other
National Park(H)
Country House

20. HUBBERHOLME
1969
Rural Other Settlement
Bulk of Settlement
Residential
National Park(H)
River

21. INGLETON
1978
Rural Main Settlement
Including Bulk of Core
Residential, Open Space, Other
National Park(H)
River

22. KETTLEWELL
1969
Rural Main Settlement,
Pre-industrial Town
Bulk of Settlement
Residential
National Park(H)
Rivers

23. LANGCLIFFE
1978
Rural Main Settlement
Bulk of Settlement
Residential
National Park(H)
Country House, Park

NORTH YORKSHIRE

24. LINTON
1969
Rural Main Settlement
Bulk of Settlement
Residential
National Park(H)
River

25. LOTHERSDALE
1979
Rural Main Settlement
Bulk of Settlement
Residential, Open Space
Stream

26. SETTLE
1972
Rural Main Settlement,
Pre-industrial Town
Including Bulk of Core
Residential, Open Space, Other
National Park(H)
Town House, Park

27. SKIPTON
1969
Town (13), Pre-industrial Town
Including Bulk of Core
Residential, Open Space, Shops/Offices
Castle, River, Mill, Woodland, Farmstead, Farmland

28. STARBOTTON
1969
Rural Main Settlement
Bulk of Settlement
Residential
National Park(H)
Stream

29. SUTTON IN CRAVEN
1980
Rural Main Settlement
Including Part of Core
Residential, Open Space, Industrial
Stream, Industrial Mill

30. THORTON IN CRAVEN
1980
Rural Main Settlement
Bulk of Settlement
Residential

31. WEST MARTON
1979
Rural Main Settlement
Bulk of Settlement
Residential

Hambleton

1. AINDERBY STEEPLE
1975
Rural Main Settlement
Bulk of Settlement
Residential
Green

2. ALNE
1985
Rural Main Settlement
Including Bulk of Core
Residential
Country House

3. BEDALE
1974
Rural Main Settlement
Including Part of Core
Residential, Other
Country House, Park, River

4. BORROWBY
1979
Rural Main Settlement
Including Bulk of Core
Residential

5. BRAFFERTON / HELPERBY
1985
Rural Main Settlements
Including Bulk of Core
Residential
Country House, Park, Formal Garden

6. CARLTON-IN-CLEVELAND
1977
Rural Main Settlement
Bulk of Settlement
Residential
National Park(E)
Stream

7. COXWOLD
1977
Rural Main Settlement
Bulk of Settlement
Residential
National Park(E)
Country House, Almshouses

8. CRAKEHALL
1976
Rural Main Settlement
Bulk of Settlement
Residential, Open Space
Country House, River, Mill, Green

9. CRAYKE
1976
Rural Main Settlement
Bulk of Settlement
Residential
A.O.N.B.(14)
Green, Country Houses

10. EASINGWOLD
1972
Rural Main Settlement
Including Bulk of Core
Residential, Other

11. GREAT AYTON
1973
Rural Main Settlement
Including Bulk of Core
Residential, Open Space, Other
River, Country Houses, Greens, Meadow

12. HUTTON RUDBY
1971
Rural Main Settlement
Bulk of Settlement
Residential
River, Country House, Woodland, Green, Moated Site

13. KIRKBY-IN-CLEVELAND
1984
Rural Main Settlement
Including Bulk of Core
Residential

14. KIRKLINGTON
1986
Rural Main Settlement
Bulk of Settlement
Residential
Green, Stream, Mill, Woodland, Country House

15. NEWBY WISKE
1986
Rural Main Settlement
Bulk of Settlement
Residential
Country House, Park, Woodland, Pond

16. OSMOTHERLEY
1977
Rural Main Settlement
Including Bulk of Core
Residential
National Park(E)

NORTH YORKSHIRE

17. SNAPE
1986
Rural Main Settlement
Bulk of Settlement
Residential
Castle

18. STILLINGTON
1976
Rural Main Settlement
Including Bulk of Core
Residential
Green, Pond

19. STOKESLEY
1971
Rural Main Settlement,
Pre-industrial Town
Including Bulk of Core
Residential, Other
River

20. SUTTON ON THE FOREST
1971
Rural Main Settlement
Bulk of Settlement
Residential
Country House, Park

21. SWAINBY
1977
Rural Main Settlement
Bulk of Settlement
Residential
National Park(E)
Deserted Medieval Village, Castle,
  Farmsteads, River, Farmland

22. THIRSK AND SOWERBY
1971
Rural Main Settlements,
Pre-industrial Town
Including Part of Core
Residential, Open Space, Other
River, Meadows, Mills, Tumulus,
Bridge, Green, Country House

23. WEST TANFIELD
1976
Rural Main Settlement
Including Bulk of Core
Residential
River

Harrogate

1. ALDBOROUGH
1976
Rural Other Settlement,
Pre-industrial Town
Bulk of Settlement
Residential
Roman Town, Country House, Park,
Meadows, Woodland

2. BISHOP MONKTON
1970
Rural Main Settlement
Including Bulk of Core
Residential
Mill

3. BOROUGHBRIDGE
1976
Rural Main Settlement,
Pre-industrial Town
Including Bulk of Core
Residential, Other
River, Country House, Canal,
Stream

4. BURTON LEONARD
1976
Rural Main Settlement
Including Bulk of Core
Residential

5. FOLLIFOOT
1979
Rural Main Settlement
Including Bulk of Core
Residential

6. GOLDSBOROUGH
1978
Rural Main Settlement
Including Bulk of Core
Residential
Country House, Park, Avenue

7. GREEN HAMMERTON
1977
Rural Main Settlement
Including Bulk of Core
Residential
Green

8. HAMPSTHWAITE
1976
Rural Main Settlement
Including Bulk of Core
Residential
River, Bridge

9. HARROGATE
1976 (1973) Amalgamated
Town (66)
Including Bulk of Core
Residential, Open Space, Shops/
Offices, Other
Common

10. KIRK DEIGHTON
1979
Rural Main Settlement
Including Bulk of Core
Residential, Open Space

11. KIRK HAMMERTON
1977
Rural Main Settlement
Including Bulk of Core
Residential

12. KNARESBOROUGH
1969
Town (13), Pre-industrial Town
Including Bulk of Core
Residential, Open Space, Shops/
Offices
River, Town House, Park, Castle,
Bridge, Mill

13. KNARESBOROUGH,
  ABBEY ROAD
1978
Urban Non Settlement (13)
Not Applicable
River, Woodland

14. MARTON-CUM-GRAFTON
1979
Rural Main Settlement
Bulk of Settlement
Residential, Open Space

15. MASHAM
1976
Rural Main Settlement,
Pre-industrial Town
Including Bulk of Core
Residential, Open Space, Other
River, Mill

16. NUN MONKTON
1973
Rural Main Settlement
Bulk of Settlement
Residential, Open Space
Common

17. PATELEY BRIDGE
1970
Rural Main Settlement,
Pre-industrial Town
Including Bulk of Core
Residential, Other
River, Mill

18. RIPLEY
1978
Rural Main Settlement
Bulk of Settlement
Residential, Open Space
Country House, Avenue

19. RIPON
1976 (1969) Amended
Town (12), Pre-industrial Town
Including Bulk of Core
Residential, Shops/Offices, Other
River

NORTH YORKSHIRE

20. ROECLIFFE
1976
Rural Main Settlement
Bulk of Settlement
Residential
Green

21. SCRIVEN
1977
Rural Main Settlement
Including Bulk of Core
Residential
Woodland

22. SPOFFORTH
1978
Rural Main Settlement
Including Bulk of Core
Residential
Castle

23. STUDLEY ROGER
1973
Rural Main Settlement
Bulk of Settlement
Residential

24. WHIXLEY
1978
Rural Main Settlement
Including Bulk of Core
Residential
Country House, Park

Richmondshire

1. ALDBROUGH ST. JOHN
1975
Rural Main Settlement
Including Bulk of Core
Residential, Open Space
Green

2. BELLERBY
1981
Rural Main Settlement
Including Bulk of Core
Residential
Green

3. BOLTON ON SWALE
1977
Rural Main Settlement
Bulk of Settlement
Residential

4. BROMPTON ON SWALE
1977
Rural Main Settlement
Including Bulk of Core
Residential
River

5. CATTERICK
1977
Rural Main Settlement
Including Bulk of Core
Residential
Stream, Green

6. CROFT
1978
Rural Main Settlement
Bulk of Settlement
Residential, Open Space
Country House, Meadow

7. DALTON
1981
Rural Main Settlement
Including Bulk of Core
Residential

8. GAYLES
1982
Rural Main Settlement
Bulk of Settlement
Residential
Farmland

9. GILLING WEST
1979
Rural Main Settlement
Including Bulk of Core
Residential
River

10. HARTFORTH
1979
Rural Other Settlement
Bulk of Settlement
Residential
Country House, Park, River

11. HUDSWELL
1980
Rural Main Settlement
Including Bulk of Core
Residential
National Park(H)

12. KIRBY HILL
1981
Rural Main Settlement
Bulk of Settlement
Residential
Farmstead

13. LEYBURN
1971
Rural Main Settlement
Including Bulk of Core
Residential, Other
Country Houses, Woodland

14. MELSONBY
1975
Rural Main Settlement
Including Bulk of Core
Residential
Stream

15. MIDDLEHAM
1974
Rural Main Settlement,
Pre-industrial Town
Bulk of Settlement
Residential, Open Space, Other
Castle, Town House, Castle Mound,
Meadows

16. MIDDLETON TYAS
1978
Rural Main Settlement
Including Bulk of Core
Residential

17. NEWSHAM
1982
Rural Main Settlement
Including Bulk of Core
Residential

18. RAVENSWORTH
1982
Rural Main Settlement
Bulk of Settlement
Residential
Castle, Farmstead, Green

19. REDMIRE
1981
Rural Main Settlement
Bulk of Settlement
Residential

20. RICHMOND
1976 (1971) Amended
Town (8), Pre-industrial Town
Including Bulk of Core
Residential, Open Space, Shops/
Offices
River, Castle, Bridge, Priory, Park,
Mill, Woodland, Farmland,
Meadows, Town House

21. RICHMOND, RICHMOND HILL
SCHOOL
1984
Town (8), Pre-industrial Town
Small Part Excluding Core
Other
Barracks

NORTH YORKSHIRE

22. SCORTON
1977
Rural Main Settlement
Including Bulk of Core
Residential
Green

23. SKEEBY
1980
Rural Main Settlement
Including Bulk of Core
Residential
Farmstead

24. SPENNITHORNE
1982
Rural Main Settlement
Bulk of Settlement
Residential
Country House, Stream

Ryedale

1. AMPLEFORTH
1977
Rural Main Settlement
Bulk of Settlement
Residential
National Park(E)
Stream

2. APPLETON-LE-MOORS
1977
Rural Main Settlement
Bulk of Settlement
Residential
National Park(E)

3. BARTON LE WILLOWS
1985
Rural Main Settlement
Bulk of Settlement
Residential
Farmsteads, Green

4. BULMER
1985
Rural Main Settlement
Bulk of Settlement
Residential
A.O.N.B.(14)
Country House

5. CLIFTON
1975
See Other
Not Applicable
Residential, Open Space, Other
Green

6. FLAXTON
1985
Rural Main Settlement
Bulk of Settlement
Residential
Green

7. HAROME
1977
Rural Main Settlement
Bulk of Settlement
Residential
Mill, River

8. HAXBY
1977
Rural Main Settlement
Including Part of Core
Residential
Green

9. HELMSLEY
1973
Rural Main Settlement,
 Pre-industrial Town
Including Bulk of Core
Residential, Other
National Park(E)
Castle, River, Meadow, Bridge,
Woodland

10. HOVINGHAM
1977
Rural Main Settlement,
Pre-industrial Town
Bulk of Settlement
Residential, Other
A.O.N.B.(14)
Country House, Park, River, Stream,
Pond

11. HUTTON-LE-HOLE
1978
Rural Main Settlement
Bulk of Settlement
Residential
National Park(E)
River

12. KIRKBYMOORSIDE
1976
Rural Main Settlement,
 Pre-industrial Town
Including Bulk of Core
Residential, Other
Meadow

13. LANGTON
1977
Rural Main Settlement
Bulk of Settlement
Residential
Country House, Stream, Green

14. LASTINGHAM
1977
Rural Main Settlement
Bulk of Settlement
Residential
National Park(E)
Stream, Country House, Meadows

15. LOCKTON
1977
Rural Main Settlement
Bulk of Settlement
Residential
National Park(E)

16. MALTON
1984 (1973) Amended
Town (4), Pre-industrial Town
Including Bulk of Core
Residential, Shops/Offices,
Industrial
Roman Fort, River

17. MARTON
1977
Rural Main Settlement
Bulk of Settlement
Residential
River, Bridge, Green, Meadow

18. MIDDLETON
1985
Rural Main Settlement
Bulk of Settlement
Residential
Farmsteads

19. NUNNINGTON
1979
Rural Main Settlement
Bulk of Settlement
Residential
A.O.N.B.(14)
Country House, River

20. OLD BYLAND
1983
Rural Main Settlement
Bulk of Settlement
Residential
National Park(E)
Country House, Farmstead

21. OLD MALTON (NR. MALTON)
1979
Urban Village (4)
Bulk of Settlement
Residential
Priory, Earthworks(Medieval
Fishponds), River

NORTH YORKSHIRE

22. OSBALDWICK
1978
Rural Main Settlement
Including Bulk of Core
Residential
Stream, Green, Farmstead

23. OSWALDKIRK
1984
Rural Main Settlement
Bulk of Settlement
Residential
National Park(E)
Country House, Woodland

24. PICKERING
1973
Town (6), Pre-industrial Town
Including Bulk of Core
Residential, Shops/Offices
Castle, Stream, Meadows, Castle Mound

25. RIEVAULX
1977
Rural Main Settlement
Bulk of Settlement
Residential
National Park(E)
Abbey, Mill, River, Meadows, Woodland, Park

26. ROSEDALE ABBEY
1977
Rural Main Settlement
Bulk of Settlement
Residential
National Park(E)
Abbey, Stream, Mill

27. SAND HUTTON
1985
Rural Main Settlement
Bulk of Settlement
Residential
Farmstead, Woodland, Stream

28. SETTRINGTON
1976
Rural Main Settlement
Bulk of Settlement
Residential, Open Space
Country House, Park, Mill, Stream

29. SHERIFF HUTTON
1978
Rural Main Settlement
Including Part of Core
Residential
Castle

30. SINNINGTON
1977
Rural Main Settlement
Bulk of Settlement
Residential
National Park(E)
Country House, River, Green, Meadows

31. SKELTON
1973
Rural Main Settlement
Including Bulk of Core
Residential
Country House

32. SLINGSBY
1977
Rural Main Settlement
Bulk of Settlement
Residential
Castle

33. STRENSALL
1979
Rural Main Settlement
Including Bulk of Core
Residential
Country House, Moated Site

34. TERRINGTON
1985
Rural Main Settlement
Bulk of Settlement
Residential, Other
A.O.N.B.(14)
Country House, Farmstead

35. THORNTON DALE
1977
Rural Main Settlement
Including Bulk of Core
Residential, Other
National Park(E)
Stream, Mill, Country House, Woodland, Park, Pond

36. WELBURN
1977
Rural Main Settlement
Bulk of Settlement
Residential
A.O.N.B.(14)

37. WESTOW
1985
Rural Main Settlement
Including Bulk of Core
Residential

38. WINTRINGHAM
1985
Rural Main Settlement
Bulk of Settlement
Residential
Stream, Farmstead

Scarborough

1. BROMPTON
1985
Rural Main Settlement
Bulk of Settlement
Residential, Other
Castle, Farmsteads, Ponds

2. BURNISTON
1977
Rural Main Settlement
Including Bulk of Core
Residential
Farmsteads, Stream

3. CAYTON
1985
Rural Main Settlement
Including Bulk of Core
Residential

4. CLOUGHTON
1977
Rural Main Settlement
Including Bulk of Core
Residential
National Park(E)
Country House, Stream

5. FILEY
1977
Town (6)
Including Bulk of Core
Residential, Open Space, Other
Seafront, Ravine, Country House

6. GRISTHORPE
1978
Rural Main Settlement
Including Bulk of Core
Residential
Country House

7. HUNMANBY
1975
Rural Main Settlement
Including Bulk of Core
Residential, Open Space, Other
Country House, Park

NORTH YORKSHIRE

8. HUTTON BUSCEL
1977
Rural Main Settlement
Bulk of Settlement
Residential, Open Space
National Park(E)
Farmland, Farmstead

9. IRTON
1984
Rural Main Settlement
Including Bulk of Core
Residential

10. LEAHOLM
1983
Rural Other Settlement
Bulk of Settlement
Residential, Open Space
National Park(E)
River, Farmsteads, Stream, Country House, Park

11. LEBBERSTON
1985
Rural Main Settlement
Including Bulk of Core
Residential
Country House

12. LYTHE
1977
Rural Main Settlement
Bulk of Settlement
Residential
National Park(E)
Country House

13. MUSTON
1976
Rural Main Settlement
Bulk of Settlement
Residential
Farmsteads

14. ROBIN HOODS BAY
1974
Rural Other Settlement
Including Bulk of Core
Residential, Open Space, Other
National Park(E)
Woodland, Cliffs, Seafront, Stream

15. RUNSWICK BAY
1974
Rural Other Settlement
Including Bulk of Core
Residential, Open Space
National Park(E)
Seafront

16. RUSTON
1985
Rural Other Settlement
Bulk of Settlement
Residential
Farmsteads

17. RUSWARP (NR. WHITBY)
1985
Urban Village (14)
Including Bulk of Core
Residential
River, Mill

18. SANDSEND
1974
Rural Other Settlement
Bulk of Settlement
Residential
National Park(E)
Streams, Seafront

19. SCALBY
1980 (1979) Amended
Town (9)
Including Bulk of Core
Residential, Other
National Park(E)

20. SCARBOROUGH
1985 (1972) Amalgamated
Town (43), Pre-industrial Town
Including Bulk of Core
Residential, Open Space, Shops/Offices
Seafront, Cliffs, Castle, Harbour, Industrial Monument(Railway Station)

21. SEAMER
1985
Rural Main Settlement, Pre-industrial Town
Including Bulk of Core
Residential
Earthworks(Manor House), Farmsteads

22. SNAINTON
1985
Rural Main Settlement
Including Bulk of Core
Residential
Farmstead

23. STAITHES
1972
Rural Other Settlement
Including Bulk of Core
Residential, Open Space, Other
National Park(E)
River, Seafront, Cliffs, Harbour

24. WHITBY
1973
Town (14), Pre-industrial Town
Including Bulk of Core
Residential, Open Space, Shops/Offices, Industrial
River, Seafront, Abbey, Cliffs, Harbour, Mill, Mudflats

25. WYKEHAM
1985
Rural Main Settlement
Bulk of Settlement
Residential
Farmsteads

Selby

1. ASKHAM BRYAN
1980
Rural Main Settlement
Bulk of Settlement
Residential

2. ASKHAM RICHARD
1975
Rural Main Settlement
Bulk of Settlement
Residential
Country House

3. BILBROUGH
1977
Rural Main Settlement
Bulk of Settlement
Residential
Country House

4. BOLTON PERCY
1980
Rural Main Settlement
Including Bulk of Core
Residential
Marsh, Farmsteads, Tithe Barn, Country House

5. BRAYTON
1969
Rural Non Settlement
Not Applicable
Farmland, Church

6. CAWOOD
1977
Rural Main Settlement
Including Bulk of Core
Residential, Other
Castle, River, Meadows, Farmstead

NORTH YORKSHIRE

7. COPMANTHORPE
1973 (1970) Amended
Rural Main Settlement
Including Bulk of Core
Residential

8. HEALOUGH
1985
Rural Main Settlement
Bulk of Settlement
Residential
Country House, Farmstead,
 Meadows

9. HEMINGBROUGH
1977
Rural Main Settlement
Including Bulk of Core
Residential

10. HESLINGTON
1969
Rural Main Settlement
Bulk of Settlement
Residential
Country House

11. HILLAM
1969
Rural Main Settlement
Including Bulk of Core
Residential
Country House

12. KIRK SMEATON
1976
Rural Main Settlement
Including Bulk of Core
Residential
River, Meadows

13. LITTLE SMEATON
1976
Rural Main Settlement
Including Bulk of Core
Residential
River, Meadows, Woodland,
 Farmsteads

14. MONK FRYSTON
1969
Rural Main Settlement
Bulk of Settlement
Residential
Country House, Park, Ponds

15. NEWTON KYME
1985
Rural Main Settlement
Bulk of Settlement
Residential
Country House, Park, River

16. RICCALL
1978
Rural Main Settlement
Including Bulk of Core
Residential

17. SAXTON
1984
Rural Main Settlement
Bulk of Settlement
Residential
Farmstead

18. SELBY
1982 (1969) Amended
Town (11), Pre-industrial Town
Including Bulk of Core
Residential, Open Space, Shops/
Offices
River, Stream

19. TADCASTER
1973
Rural Main Settlement,
 Pre-industrial Town
Including Bulk of Core
Residential, Industrial, Other
River, Castle, Mill

20. THROGANBY
1977
Rural Main Settlement
Bulk of Settlement
Residential
Country House

21. WENTBRIDGE
1981
See Other
Not Applicable
Residential, Open Space
River, Meadows

22. WHELDRAKE
1979
Rural Main Settlement
Including Bulk of Core
Residential

23. WOMERSLEY
1985
Rural Main Settlement
Bulk of Settlement
Residential
Country House, Woodland

York

1. ACOMB
1975 (1968) Amalgamated
Town (100), Pre-industrial Town
Small Part Excluding Core
Residential, Open Space, Other

2. CENTRAL
1975 (1968) Amended
Town (100), Pre-industrial Town
Including Bulk of Core
Residential, Open Space, Shops/
Offices, Industrial, Other
City Wall, Castle, Cathedral
Precinct, River, Abbey, Industrial
Monument (Railway Station)

3. CLIFTON
1975 (1968) Amended
Town (100), Pre-industrial Town
Large Part Excluding Core
Residential, Open Space, Other

4. FULFORD
1975
Town (100), Pre-industrial Town
Small Part Excluding Core
Residential

5. HEWORTH / HEWORTH GREEN
1975
Town (100), Pre-industrial Town
Small Part Excluding Core
Residential

6. MIDDLETHORPE (NR. YORK)
1975
Urban Village (100)
Bulk of Settlement
Residential
Country House, Park

7. NEW WALK / TERRY AVENUE
1975
Urban Non Settlement (100)
Not Applicable
River

8. ST. PAULS SQUARE / HOLGATE
ROAD
1975
Town (100), Pre-industrial Town
Small Part Excluding Core
Residential

9. TADCASTER ROAD
1975
Town (100), Pre-industrial Town
Large Part Excluding Core
Residential, Open Space
Common

10. THE RACECOURSE / TERRYS
FACTORY
1975
Town (100), Pre-industrial Town
Small Part Excluding Core
Industrial, Other
Grandstand

NORTH YORKSHIRE

11. THE RETREAT - HESLINGTON
    ROAD
    1975
    Town (100), Pre-industrial Town
    Small Part Excluding Core
    Open Space, Other

DESIGNATION ACTIVITY 1987

Hambleton	24	NORTHALLERTON	
	25	HUSTHWAITE	
	26	ROMANBY	
	27	KIRKBY FLEETHAM	
	28	BROMPTON	
Ryedale	6	FLAXTON	(EXTENSION)
York	2	YORK CENTRAL	(EXTENSION)

DESIGNATION ACTIVITY 1988

Hambleton	29	CARLTON HUSTHWAITE	
	30	THIMBLEBY	
	3	BEDALE	(EXTENSION)
	11	GREAT AYTON	(EXTENSION)
	19	STOKESLEY	(EXTENSION)
Richmondshire	25	ASKRIGG (YORKSHIRE DALES NATIONAL PARK DESIGNATION)	
	26	LEYBURN, QUARRY HILLS HOUSE	
Ryedale	39	ALLERSTON	
	40	AISLABY	
	41	CLAXTON	
	42	BARTON-LE-STREET	

FOOTNOTES

Craven

14. EASTBY	Only that portion of the Conservation Area north of the village street lies within the National Park.
15. EMBSAY	Only that portion of the Conservation Area to the north and west of West Lane / Main Street and Kirk Lane lies within the National Park.
21. INGLETON	Only marginal portions of the Conservation Area lie within the National Park.
26. SETTLE	Only marginal portions of the Conservation Area lie within the National Park.

NORTH YORKSHIRE

FOOTNOTES continued ...

Hambleton

21. SWAINBY	The Conservation Area includes the hamlet of Whorlton, SWAINBY being the main settlement of Whorlton Civil Parish.

Harrogate

3. BOROUGHBRIDGE	This Conservation Area extends into Hambleton, NORTH YORKSHIRE.
9. HARROGATE	Amalgamating HIGH HARROGATE (1973) and LOW HARROGATE (1973).
17. PATELEY BRIDGE	This is the main settlement of High and Low Bishopside Civil Parish.

Ryedale

1. AMPLEFORTH	That portion of the designated area north of the village street occurs within the North Yorkshire National Park: the area to the south lies within the boundaries of the Howardian Hills AONB.
5. CLIFTON	See York, NORTH YORKSHIRE.
23. OSWALDKIRK	Only that portion of the designated area north of the village street occurs within the National Park. The area to the south occurs within the Howardian Hills AONB.
30. SINNINGTON	The northern section of the village lies within the National Park.

Scarborough

4. CLOUGHTON	Only a marginal portion of the Conservation Area lies within the National Park.
18. SANDSEND	Only a marginal portion of the Conservation Area lies within the National Park.
19. SCALBY	Only a marginal portion of the Conservation Area lies within the National Park.
20. SCARBOROUGH	Amalgamating NORTHERN HEADLAND (1972), TOWN CENTRE (1972) and ROYAL CRESCENT, SCARBOROUGH (1972).
23. STAITHES	This Conservation Area extends into Langbaurgh, CLEVELAND.

Selby

12. KIRK SMEATON	Portion 'B' of LITTLE SMEATON Conservation Area relates to the KIRK SMEATON designation. A small eastern extension of the latter relates to the LITTLE SMEATON designation and lies on the Doncaster - South Yorkshire boundary.
21. WENTBRIDGE	See also Wakefield, WEST YORKSHIRE.

York

2. CENTRAL	Amalgamating FRONT STREET (1968) and ACOMB GREEN (1968).
3. CLIFTON	This Conservation Area extends into Ryedale, NORTH YORKSHIRE.

GLOSSARY OF TERMS

1. Conservation area

Conservation areas were first introduced under Section 1 of the Civic Amenities Act, 1967. Under this Act, all local planning authorities were required to determine which parts of their areas were of special architectural or historic interest, the character of appearance of which it was desirable to preserve or enhance, and they were required to designate these as conservation areas. Designation therefore is more than a statement of fact, it is also one of policy. The relevant section is now S277 of the Town and Country Planning Act, 1971.

In 1974, responsibility for designation was transferred from the county councils and county boroughs to the new district authorities though provision was made for the county councils to designate following consultations with the districts. In the national parks, the relevant designating authorities remain the county councils operating, where necessary, through special national park joint committees. The Lake District and Peak District however are planning authorities in their own right with their own planning boards. In London, the Greater London Council retained its power to designate and in 1986 this passed to the Historic Buildings and Monuments Commission for England (English Heritage). But designation is primarily the duty of the London boroughs. Following the 1980 Act which led to the creation of Urban Development Corporations, the London Docklands and Merseyside Development Corporations received powers to designate.

Section 28 of the 1971 Act contains a special procedure for dealing with applications for planning permission for the development of land in or adjacent to a conservation area if the local planning authority is of the opinion that the development would affect the character of appearance of the area.

Section 277A brings the demolition of buildings in conservation areas under control: conservation area consent must be sought for proposals involving the demolition of part or all of any building other than a listed building. For the latter listed building consent must be obtained for both demolition and material alternations.

Section 61A extends control over trees. Any person wishing to cut down or carry out works to a tree is required to give the local planning authority six weeks notice to enable the authority to consider whether to make a tree preservation order.

In the Inventory, conservation areas are listed by name under the London borough, metropolitan or shire district in which they occur. This applies even to those areas designated by national park authorities and urban development corporations. Only those areas designated prior to 1987 are shown in the main Inventory. Later designations and amendments are listed separately.

The name shown is that given on designation, but where the area is located in a town the name of the town is shown and areas occurring in a particular town are grouped together in the Inventory. A conservation area which lies within an urban area (see below for definition) but not in a town is shown as 'near' the town found in that urban area.

2. **Date**

The year shown is the year in which the designation notice appeared in the London Gazette. The actual date of designation may in some instances have occurred in the previous year. Where the conservation area has been amended, or where two or more areas have been amalgamated, the latest date in which either event may have occurred is shown and the date of the earliest designation of any part of the area is shown in brackets. In one or two instances, de-designation has subsequently occurred: this is recorded in the Inventory in the notes to the relevant county.

A conservation area designation may comprise several distinct areas. Where there is doubt as to whether this applied at the time of designation the areas are shown as separate designations.

3. **Urban areas and their population**

An 'urban area' is a local government pre-reorganisation (pre 1974) urban administrative unit (Greater London and London boroughs, county and municipal boroughs and urban districts). Where conservation areas occur in urban areas, the 1981 population of the urban area in question is shown in brackets in '000s.

4. **Location**

(a) London

The term is not precise but refers to the main, continuously built-up area existing within the Greater London urban area.

(b) Town/Twin Town

A town is the main built-up area occurring in an urban area. It normally possesses a commercial nucleus with shopping streets. London however is excluded from this definition. Occasionally more than one substantial built-up area with a commercial nucleus occurs within an urban area and in such instances, the term 'twin town' is used. This draws attention to the fact that the population shown may not relate solely or mainly to the town in which the conservation area occurs.

(c)   Urban village

This is a settlement which lacks a commercial nucleus but which is located in an urban area. It is generally a village but can comprise a built-up area or a blend of the two.

(d)   Urban non-settlement

A 'non-settlement' is a feature, usually associated with a number of buildings such as a farmstead or country house. Even though the buildings may be used for habitation, if the feature is the dominant element the term 'non-settlement' is applied. The above term refers to a 'non-settlement' located in an urban area.

(e)   Rural settlement

These are settlements occurring within rural areas, that is, pre-reorganisation Rural Districts. The vast majority are villages but some have the characteristics of small towns. The main settlement of a civil parish is referred to as a 'Rural Main Settlement'. Any other settlement in a civil parish is identified as a 'Rural Other Settlement'.

Occasionally substantial built-up areas occur within rural areas or extend into them from adjacent towns. The most notable examples are some of the new towns. Bracknell, Hatfield and Peterlee lie entirely within rural areas; substantial portions of Aycliffe, Warrington, Milton Keynes, Telford, and Central Lancashire new towns also occur within rural areas. But these and other built-up areas are rarely designated.

(f)   Rural non-settlement

A 'non-settlement' occurring in a rural area (see 'Urban non-settlement').

(g)   'See other'

Occasionally a conservation area relates to a settlement or feature which extends across a district or county boundary. Though two or more designations are necessary, this is due entirely to the presence of the administrative boundary; in any other circumstances only one conservation area would be designated. There will therefore be more than one entry in the inventory but each will relate to the relevant area as a whole. But only one entry will give location information (i.e. 'town'; 'rural settlement'; etc), the other/s will be marked 'see other'. Statistics relating to the numbers of conservation areas will exclude 'see other' entries.

Whilst each authority should have specifically designated their portion of the area, formal designation does not always appear to have occurred and 'second entries' may not be listed. However details of the other relevant authority are given in all cases.

5. **Pre-industrial town**

In the pre-industrial period (before about 1750) settlements, which were towns, could generally be distinguished by their urban form. This normally included an area set aside for a market; burgage plots and town defences were also typical morphological characteristics. Urban status was usually emphasised by a borough charter. In 1972, the Council for British Archaeology published a study edited by Carolyn Heighway under the title 'The Erosion of History' which identified the pre-industrial towns of Britain. Further urban research since that time could results in the list being extended, but it is used in its original form in this inventory as the basis for defining pre-industrial towns.

For our purposes the full extent of a contemporary town, urban village or rural settlement which has grown directly and continuously from a pre-industrial town is termed a 'pre-industrial town'. This applies even where the historic nucleus does not coincide completely with the modern town's commercial nucleus; it also applies where there are two commercial nuclei of which only one is pre-industrial in origin. In one instance - Old Sarum - the former medieval town now exists as an 'urban non-settlement'. Abandoned roman town sites are discounted.

The term 'pre-industrial' town does not necessarily imply that the conservation area occurs within the site of the pre-industrial township, only that it occurs within a town or other settlement which itself has pre-industrial urban roots.

About half of all towns, along with over 300 rural settlements/urban villages, have 'pre-industrial town' origins. Towns not having pre-industrial urban roots can conveniently be referred to as '19th century'. Most are to be found in, or close to, the metropolitan areas, but the group also includes inland spas like Malvern and seaside resorts like Brighton, Southport and Blackpool. Major industrial centres outside the metropolitan areas like Middlesbrough and Barrow-in-Furness are also included. Nineteenth century towns are also associated with railway centres like Swindon and Crewe. Of the nineteenth century towns Birmingham is the largest. The most recent are the garden cities of Letchworth and Welwyn, both strictly of early twentieth century origin.

Within London, pre-industrial towns occurred at a number of locations apart from the City and Westminster. They relate to existing commercial nuclei at Croydon, Barking, Bromley, Enfield, Harrow, Orpington, Romford, Southwark and Uxbridge, all of which have been partially designated. Further 'towns' existed at Brentford and Chipping Barnet.

'Pre-industrial towns' are therefore modern settlements with pre-industrial urban roots; but as London cannot be divided into meaningful settlements, the relationship between London's pre-industrial towns and its conservation areas cannot be fully expressed and references to pre-industrial towns in London have been excluded from the inventory.

6. **Location and extent within settlement**

A number of terms are employed to indicate the location of the conservation area within the town, urban village or rural settlement in which it occurs and its extent with respect either to the core (see below) or to the settlement as a whole. No attempt has been made to do this in London where neither the local commercial cores nor the specific areas relating to them are readily definable. London borough boundaries are of little relevance in this connection, for example, a number of shopping centres actually sit astride these boundaries.

In towns, some authorities have tended to designate a single conservation area whilst others have designated a number of abutting areas. The former would be shown perhaps as including the bulk of the core whereas each of the latter would appear as including no more than a part of the core. The overall area designated, however, could actually be the same. In short, the information given relates to the conservation area, not to the town.

(a)   Core : with reference to towns

The term implies the main commercial nucleus - the 'town centre'. This will include the main shopping streets and public buildings. It may include land in educational, religious and civic use but not primarily residential areas. In some cases, the town in question may have more than one commercial nucleus.

(b)   Core : with reference to urban villages and rural settlements

The term here implies the traditional settlement and would normally include the whole of the pre-1914 settlement.

(c)   Bulk of settlement

This term is employed in the inventory where by far the greater portion of the settlement is included within the conservation area. Such a situation rarely, if ever, occurs in a town. It tends to apply to the smallest rural settlements. Where the conservation area extends into open countryside, this will be indicated by an associated reference to topographical features such as farmland, moorland etc.

(d)   Bulk of core

This implies that by far the greater part of the core is included within the conservation area. In towns, where housing or other areas are also covered, this will be shown as 'residential' etc. under the 'land use' heading. Any further extension into open countryside will be indicated by a reference to farmland, woodland, meadows etc.

(e)   Part of core

This implies that only a minority of the core is included in the conservation area.

(f)   Large/small part excluding core

This condition tends to occur only in towns. The term refers to situations where the conservation area lies wholly outside the core. The words 'large' and 'small' are relative to the size of the town in which the conservation area occurs. In the largest towns however, the terms primarily distinguish the extent of the areas relative to each other.

7.   **Land Use**

Various urban land uses are distinguished, that is, uses related to towns, urban villages, rural settlements and to the built-up area of London. Even an area which is not a settlement may include an urban land use of some kind. Five categories are distinguished: residential; open space; shops/offices; industrial; and 'other'.

(a)   Residential

This implies that the conservation area or part of it comprises housing development. 'Residential' is a broad term which embraces minor pockets in shopping, ecclesiastical, educational use etc, particularly in villages.

(b)   Open space

This implies open space for recreational use. In most cases this will be public open space such as urban parks. Cemeteries are not included, nor are wider areas of open countryside however accessible these may be to public use.

(c)   Shops/offices

This term can imply shops or offices, or both. But, apart from in London, the term is employed in the inventory only in relation to the 'cores' of towns. An exception is made for 17 towns, chiefly in Shropshire, which lost their urban status shortly before local government re-organisation in 1974.

'Shops/offices' includes buildings closely associated with the town centre such as railway stations, car parks, public buildings, churches etc.

In rural settlements, especially in pre-industrial towns, whole streets in shopping use sometimes occur, in effect 'high streets'. These are shown as 'other' (see below) rather than as 'shops/offices'.

(d)   Industrial

This term applies to areas of industrial character and major buildings designed for industrial use. The degree to which this use is currently active is not taken into account. Major docks may be shown as 'industrial' even where they are no longer in use.

(e)   Other

Major areas in ecclesiastical, hospital, educational or other use are shown as 'other'. This is particularly the case where these uses constitute the only land use. The term is also used for shopping streets which constitute local centres in towns and also those in rural settlements. But village shops, small village schools and churches are not shown as 'other'. Instead they are implied by the term 'core' and, in particular, 'bulk of core' or 'bulk of settlement'.

8. **National Parks and Areas of Outstanding Natural Beauty**

Where a conservation area, or part of it, occurs in a national park or area of outstanding natural beauty, the name of the National Park or AONB is given. Special legislation, grant-aid, administrative arrangements and management policies apply in the parks and AONBs. Conservation areas wholly or partly within the New Forest are also indicated.

A small number of 'heritage coasts' have been defined for which special arrangements exist but these have not been separately shown in the Inventory as with the exception of four headlands, they tend to occur within the areas of AONBs which are already noted.

Each national park and area of outstanding natural beauty is coded in the inventory as follows:

National Parks and New Forest

A	Dartmoor	B	Exmoor
C	Lake District	D	New Forest
E	North York Moors	F	Northumberland
G	Peak District	H	Yorkshire Dales

Areas of Outstanding Natural Beauty

1	Arnside and Silverdale	2	Cannock Chase
3	Chichester Harbour	4	Chilterns
5	Cornwall	6	Cotswolds
7	Cranborne Chase and West Wiltshire Downs		
8	Dedham Vale	9	Dorset
10	East Devon	11	East Hampshire
12	Forest of Bowland	13	High Weald
14	Howardian Hills	15	Isles of Scilly
16	Isle of Wight	17	Kent Downs
18	Lincolnshire Wolds	19	Malvern Hills
20	Mendip Hills	21	Norfolk Coast
22	North Devon	23	North Pennines
24	North Wessex Downs	25	Northumberland Coast
26	Quantock Hills	27	Shropshire Hills
28	Solway Coast	29	South Devon
30	South Hampshire Coast	31	Suffolk Coast and Heaths
32	Surrey Hills	33	Sussex Downs
34	Wye Valley		

9. **Special features**

(a) Built features

Certain categories of built feature are noted; also shown are those features which appear, from the shape and extent of the conservation area, to have been purposefully included as important. It must be stressed that these features will not necessarily equate with outstanding listed buildings. The following are examples of the types of built features which frequently appear in rural designations:-

country houses
farmsteads, mills and other agricultural features
features of archaeological interest
defensive features
ecclesiastical features
features of civic and institutional interest
features associated with industry and transport

The features shown will not necessarily be in use today as a country house or farmstead or mill.

Within town conservation areas, major areas of specialist character may be shown as built features, for instance a cathedral precinct or a large dockyard or barracks.

Parish churches in towns and villages constitute important built features, but their presence within designated areas, especially in rural settlements, is so prevalent that there seemed little need to itemise them individually.

Planned communities and industrial communities are treated as built features: they include places like Saltaire near Bradford, Swindon Railway Village and the pioneering layouts of Letchworth and Welwyn Garden Cities.

Most conservation areas within the 'non-settlement' group are based on built features or, more rarely, on a topographical feature of some sort (see below).

(b)   Topographical features

Many conservation areas extend beyond the limits of the settlement to include an area of open country. A broad indication of the nature of this open country is given, for example:-

>   farmland
>   meadows
>   uncultivated countryside (common, moor, heath, marsh, woodland)
>   park (normally linked to a country house, not a town park)
>   water (river, pond, lake)
>   coastal (estuary, cliffs, seafront, harbour)

Water and coastal features are shown where they abut, as well as where they occur within, a conservation area. In some instances, minor streams, which help to identify the limits of the conservation area, are noted even though they do not constitute significant topographical features.